Robotization of Work?

Robotization of Work?

Answers from Popular Culture, Media and Social Sciences

Barbara Czarniawska

Senior Professor of Management, GRI, School of Business, Economics and Law, University of Gothenburg, Sweden

Bernward Joerges

Professor Dr Emeritus, Institute of Sociology, Technical University Berlin and WZB, Berlin Social Science Center, Germany

 Edward Elgar
PUBLISHING

Cheltenham, UK • Northampton, MA, USA

Original artwork: Musical Life, 1916 by Lyubov Popova.

Published by
Edward Elgar Publishing Limited
The Lypiatts
15 Lansdown Road
Cheltenham
Glos GL50 2JA
UK

Edward Elgar Publishing, Inc.
William Pratt House
9 Dewey Court
Northampton
Massachusetts 01060
USA

Paperback edition 2021

A catalogue record for this book
is available from the British Library

Library of Congress Control Number: 2020931689

This book is available electronically in the **Elgar**online
Business subject collection
DOI 10.4337/9781839100956

MIX
Paper from
responsible sources
FSC
www.fsc.org   FSC® C013056

ISBN 978 1 83910 094 9 (cased)
ISBN 978 1 83910 095 6 (eBook)
ISBN 978 1 80088 247 8 (paperback)

Printed and bound in Great Britain by TJ Books Limited, Padstow, Cornwall

Contents

Acknowledgements

The authors would like to thank Stiftelsen för ekonomisk forskning i Västsverige for its financial support; our friend and excellent language editor, Nina Lee Colwill, for her fantastic job with our text; the members of Managing Digital Transformation program at GRI for their feedback; and Melodie Ebner-Joerges for her intellectual and emotional support.

1. Introduction

> ... we no longer live in the Age of Reason. We do not have reason; we have computation. We don't have a tree of knowledge; we have an information superhighway. We don't have real intelligence; we have artificial intelligence. We no longer pursue truth, we seek data and signals. We no longer have philosophers, we have thinking pragmatists. We no longer have morals, we have lifestyles. We no longer have brains that serve as the seat of our thinking minds; we have neural sites, which remember, store body signals, control genes, generate dreams, anxieties and neuroses, quite independent of whether they think rationally or not. (...) We need to know there are machines that are cleverer than we are, so none of our systems of knowledge function as complete explanations of anything, and our understanding is always a partial phenomenon.
>
> (Malcolm Bradbury, *To the Hermitage*, 2000: 193)

A correct diagnosis? A dystopian prediction? Both? As "thinking pragmatists," we decided to dip into other descriptions of robotization – which is more visible now than it was when Bradbury wrote his *magnum opus*. In order to paint a comprehensive picture, we looked at science fiction, at the media, and at social science, all of which are closely connected.

It was Czech author Karel Čapek who, in 1920, coined the term "robot" (from *robota*, "labor" in Slavic languages; *robotnik* means "worker"). In his play, *R.U.R, Rossum Universal Robots*, artificial humans made of synthetic organic materials worked in factories, and developed lives that were not substantially different from those of the people.[1]

R.U.R. became a science fiction classic between World War I and World War II, and its topics were taken up with great enthusiasm in the 1950s and 1960s. The Cold War found expression in space competition, among other things. Cybernetics and cyborgs seemed to be an inescapable future, initially in space travels, but later even in industrial production. The matter was so serious that by 1942, Isaac Asimov had already formulated his Three Laws of Robotics, meant to keep humanoid machines in their place subordinate to humans. Although it was fiction,

---

[1] Machines doing things existed before Čapek's work (see e.g. Edgar A. Poe's essay on "Maelzel's chess player" from 1836, and more recently Riskin, 2016), but they were not meant to perform actual work.

it has been taken extremely seriously by artificial intelligence (AI) researchers and others.

When the Iron Curtain fell, space travel lost its attraction, but robots entered production processes in many industries. The end of the 1970s had seen the latest of recurring debates about automation, technological unemployment, and deskilling, triggered by Braverman's book (1974), but it had faded out in the 1980s.

Now the debate is back. "Robots could take half of the jobs in Germany." Serious authors write either enthusiastic or dystopic books about robotization. (John Searle critically reviewed two in 2014: Floridi's enthusiastic *The Fourth Revolution* and Boström's dystopic *Superintelligence* from the same year, protesting that computers will never develop a consciousness.) We are apparently witnessing a "robot revolution" – or so such serious sources as Bank of America Merrill Lynch investigators claim. In the next seven chapters, we analyze the fears and hopes occasioned by automation, as reflected in popular culture from the coining of the term "robot" to the present media hype. Have such hopes and fears changed? If so, did the changes reflect actual changes in robotics, or do robotics remain the same?

We limit the scope of our investigation by adopting the definition of robots suggested by Danica Kragic, a professor at the Royal Institute of Technology in Stockholm (see e.g. Bütepage and Kragic, 2017). According to her, robots are machines that possess a physical body and are equipped with sensors and motors or actuators. Artificial Intelligence (AI) is learning software that processes information collected by the robot's sensors, thus permitting it to work. In this sense, advanced robots are dependent on AI, but not all AI software serves robots. (Kragic tends to look too far into the future here, however. After all, a great many industrial robots were and are *automatic* robots, operated by simple programs that are unable to learn. It is only now that the number of AI-steered robots – *autonomous* robots – is growing.)

We have chosen to include popular culture in our inquiry because we believe it has a greater impact on public opinion than the social sciences (more on that in the section, "Robotization and popular culture"). But considering the enormity of the material involved (novels, films, comics, etc.), we chose only the groundbreaking works – those which were undoubtedly popular practically all over the world. Some of them have become widely popular only after having been remade into movies. They all belong to the genre known as science fiction, or its close cousin, "speculative fiction."[2]

We begin by tracking down possible sources of the present media hype – reports on ongoing robotization of work.

---

[2] A term allegedly coined by Robert Heinlein (Asimov, 1981) but used to describe works of e.g. Ursula Le Guin and Margaret Atwood.

2. Robot revolution?

The media hype likely took off in the wake of Carl Benedikt Frey and Michael A. Osborne's work. After having organized an Oxford workshop on "Machines and Employment" on September 17, 2013, they published a report called "The future of employment: How susceptible are jobs to computerisation?" Quoting, among others, Brynjolfsson and McAfee's 2011 book and McKinsey's Global Institute Report from 2013, which suggested that sophisticated algorithms can replace some 140 million knowledge workers, they examined the expected impact of computerization on US labor markets.

Having scrutinized the increasing role played by technology in economics, Frey and Osborne noted that the original fears about technological unemployment, such as those formulated by Ricardo in 1819, were exaggerated, because "technological progress has two competing effects on employment" (p. 13):

> First, as technology substitutes for labour, there is a destruction effect, requiring workers to reallocate their labour supply; and second, there is a capitalisation effect, as more companies enter industries where productivity is relatively high, leading employment in those industries to expand. (Frey and Osborne, 2013: 13)

Until now, Frey and Osborne continued, human workers have been ahead of machines because of their ability to learn; yet recent developments in artificial intelligence (AI) research suggest that digital machines can surpass the human ability to learn. Historically, machines have replaced people in manual and routine tasks; at present, they begin to undertake such non-routine, cognitive tasks as driving cars. This feat is possible primarily "due to efforts to turn non-routine tasks into well-defined problems" (p. 15), which, in turn, is facilitated by the accessibility of Big Data and the use of sophisticated algorithms.

Frey and Osborne admitted that their study mainly estimated the destruction effect, but they claimed that it also indicated possible fields in which the capitalization effect may be stronger. Having analyzed 702 occupations, they concluded that 47 percent of US employment is potentially automatable within the next decade or two – which would bring us to the first half of the 2030s. Some of these results are unsurprising, as the expected growth in automation concerns transportation, logistics, production, and administrative support. Digital bureaucracy is obviously on the rise (Czarniawska, 2019).

The authors expressed greater surprise at the trend in services, sales, and construction being similar to the trend in transportation, logistics, production, and administrative support. They also claimed that the present wave of automation would be followed by a slowdown caused by engineering bottlenecks. The jobs requiring superior perception and manipulation would be saved, they contended, until robotic competence increases in earnest. The greatest resistance to robotization, they maintained, will be in "generalist occupations requiring knowledge of human heuristics, and specialist occupations involving the development of novel ideas and artifacts" (Frey and Osborne, 2013: 40).

Frey and Osborne also discussed the limitations of their findings. Robotization will proceed when and where cheaper human labor is unavailable. Regulations and political actions may shape (facilitate or constrain) robotization differently in different geographical locations. Finally, they apologized for using such vague terms as "in a decade or two," explaining that "making predictions about technological progress is notoriously difficult" (p. 43). As an example, they quoted Marvin Minsky's 1970 statement: "in from three to eight years we will have a machine with the general intelligence of an average human being." We can add that Hans Moravec claimed in 1988 that "in 20 years" it would be possible to transfer the human brain into a plastic body (Joerges, 1989). Apparently, he still says that.

Other reports followed suit. Sweden's *Stiftelse för strategisk forskning* (Foundation for Strategic Research) asked economist Stefan Fölster (2014) to apply Frey and Osborne's method to Swedish data on 109 occupations. The results indicated that 53 percent of Swedish employment may be automatized within two decades, partly because Sweden has many industrial jobs that haven't been robotized. The people least threatened appeared to be foresters, priests, and specialized teachers; most threatened were cashiers, sellers, and machine operators (also photo models, but there are not many of them). In contrast to many works of popular fiction, police workers are unlikely to be replaced by robots, whereas bookkeepers and accountants are highly likely (46 percent) to be replaced. Additionally, and in agreement with Frey and Osborne's list of limitations, Swedish economic reforms kept unemployment at bay, as has also happened in Germany and Switzerland, but not, according to Fölster, in Italy or France.

On February 18, 2015, Dagobert Brito and Robert Curl from James A. Baker III Institute for Public Policy at Rice University published a report entitled "Turing robots: Income inequality and social mobility." ("Turing robots" refers to an automation technology that displaces a human worker.) They acknowledged the impact of both Frey and Osborne's report and Brynjolfsson and McAfee's book, but their data were taken mostly from Piketty (2014). The groundwork for Brito and Curl's report was the observation that the top 10 percent of the population earned 32 percent of labor income in 1970, but in 2012 they earned 47 percent – a change that the authors attributed to automation. Their interpretation went against the optimistic one, which sees automation as a creative destruction that will lead to new jobs:

> The machine age replaced muscle power with machines. However, until 1980 machines still needed human brains to operate and guide them, and the total number of jobs increased with growing production. *The second machine age is replacing human brains in tasks that can be reduced to an algorithm. It will be difficult to replace the jobs lost to computers.* (Brito and Curl, 2015: 4, italics in original)

They defined "robots" as "Turing robots," suggesting that they meant autonomous robots and not merely automated robots. Comparing the growth in Turing robots to growing income inequality, they concluded that if the number of robots increases at the same pace as it was increasing at the time of their writing, the top 10 percent of the population would be earning 130 percent more that the remaining 90 percent by 2040. The only good thing about such increased robotization is, in the opinion of the authors, that the "demographic problem of too few young workers to support the elderly will be solved" (p. 35).

The jobs that remain with humans will have to be jobs that computers cannot do, that require skills relatively scarce among the humans, yet common enough to employ a significant portion of the population. As to income inequality, a substantial retribution for the unemployed masses – most likely in the form of transfer payments – will be necessary.

The authors ended their report in a vein similar to that of Frey and Osborne, by saying that an unpredicted technological change may turn their predictions upside down, but that "work and education are essential to maintaining a healthy society, and this will not change" (p. 36).

Brito and Curl's text was actually presented as a research paper, whereas Bank of America Merrill Lynch's "Robot revolution – global robot & AI primer" (December 16, 2015) was a report on reports: thus the "primer" in the title. Compiled by three "Equity Strategists" from UK (Beija Ma, Sarbjit Nahal, and Felix Tran), it contains a review of the reports on robots and AI that were the most relevant up until 2015.

In the opinion of the analysts, robots would be performing 45 percent of manufacturing tasks by 2025; at the time of their writing, the figure was 10 percent. They contended that such a level of robotization could boost productivity in many industries by 30 percent, while cutting production costs by 18–33 percent. (Observe the uncertain estimate.) The authors agreed with the previous reports discussed here on both the displacement of human labor and the growth in inequality. They admitted problems related to cyber security, privacy, and possibly "killer robots." Nevertheless, consistent with their interest as bank employees, they indicated eight, albeit redundant, areas of importance to investors:

1. AI (machine learning, elaboration of Big Data): "There is a 50% chance of full AI (high-level machine learning) by 2040-50 and a 90% chance by 2075 according to AI researchers" (p. 4).
2. Industrials (automation, industrial internet, robots): "There is huge scope for growth with robot penetration in industry at only 66 robots per 10,000 workers worldwide"[1] (p. 5). They indicated massive differences from country to country, with Japan in the lead.
3. Autos and transport (autonomous vehicles – AVs): "Currently, only the US, the UK, Japan, Germany, France, Sweden and Singapore have permitted testing of AVs. An insurance framework needs to be developed addressing responsibility for collisions" (p. 6).
4. Aerospace and defense (unmanned systems, military drones, robots, and AI): "Stakeholders, including experts in AI, lawyers and activists are also expressing growing concern that growing reliance on cheap drones, the lack of human control and unpredictable/'stupid' AI could pose a threat from 'killer robots,' as expressed at an October 2015 UN conference" (p. 7).
5. Financials (robo-advisors, AI and robo-analysts, automated trading systems): "Robots and automated systems will complement rather than replace humans in financial services in our view" (p. 8); 43

---

[1] One could wonder how they counted robots. Obviously, all such predictions are highly speculative.

percent of finance executives believed that technology complicates communication, creating errors (a bear market during the financial crisis or Flash Crash caused by errors in robotrading).

6. Healthcare (medical robots, computer-assisted surgery, care-bots): Global aging and increasing per capita expenditures in Emerging Markets countries will drive growth in this area. "Japan is leading the way with one-third of the government budget on robots devoted to the elderly" (p. 9).

7. Service (care-bots, companions, domestic help, education, entertainment, security): In the USA, household robots sell the most, followed by toy robots. The next fast-growth areas include assistance for elderly and disabled people, and personal security and surveillance (p. 10).

8. Agriculture (agribots, drones, unmanned aerial vehicles): "Up to 80% of the commercial market for drones could eventually be dedicated to agriculture" (p. 11).

The summary of various reports ends with a note on the analysts' surprise concerning weak predictions for robotization of the mining industry.

In December 2016, the Executive Office of the US President Barack Obama published a report entitled "Artificial intelligence, automation, and the economy." It begins with a statement that AI-driven automation has great potential economic benefits, but that these benefits will not necessarily be evenly distributed throughout society. Like us, the authors of the report compared "then" – the twentieth century with "now" – the early twenty-first century. The automation of this first époque raised the productivity of lower-skilled workers. Current automation raised the productivity of more highly skilled workers, threatening routine-intensive occupations. The future is hard to predict, as "AI is not a single technology, but rather a collection of technologies" (p. 2). The authors agreed with Frey and Osborne, who were among the scholars quoted. It appears as well that one of the trends that began in the twentieth century continues: "Research continuously finds that the jobs that are threatened by automation are highly concentrated among lower-paid, lower-skilled, and less-educated workers" (p. 2). Yet "[t]echnology is not destiny; economic incentives and public policy can play a significant role in shaping the direction and the effects of technological change" (p. 3). The report suggests three strategies: (1) investing in fields like cyberdefense and the detection of fraudulent transactions and messages, in which AI is undoubtedly beneficial; (2) preparing US citizens for the necessity of continuous education; and (3) helping workers in transition by modernizing the social safety net. It ends with:

> If job displacements from AI are considerably beyond the patterns of technological change previously observed in economic history, a more aggressive policy response would likely be needed, with policymakers potentially exploring countervailing job creation strategies, new training supports, a more robust safety net, or additional strategies to combat inequality. (p. 42)

It is unlikely that the present (2020) US Office of the President will adopt these conclusions.

There were also many surveys, like the US think tank, Pew Research Center's, "AI, robotics, and the future of jobs" (Smith and Anderson, August 6, 2014); *Edge's* "What do you think about machines that think?" (January 26, 2015); and the World Economic Forum's (WEF) "The future of jobs: Employment, skills and workforce strategy for the fourth industrial revolution" (January 18, 2016). The Preface to the WEF report ends with a summary of the conclusions of other surveys: "The current technological revolution need not become a race between humans and machines but rather an opportunity for work to truly become a channel through which people recognize their full potential." In all three surveys, the respondents were neatly divided between the two opinions.

Pew Research Center's collaborators, Aaron Smith and Janna Anderson (2014), summarized the key findings of the survey in which 1,896 experts, 84 percent of whom were from North America, responded to the question: "The economic impact of robotic advances and AI— Self-driving cars, intelligent digital agents that can act for you, and robots are advancing rapidly. Will networked, automated, artificial intelligence (AI) applications and robotic devices have displaced more jobs than they have created by 2025?" The authors identified several key themes:

Key themes: reasons to be hopeful
1. Advances in technology may displace certain types of work, but historically they have been a net creator of jobs.
2. We will adapt to these changes by inventing entirely new types of work, and by taking advantage of uniquely human capabilities.

3.   Technology will free us from day-to-day drudgery, and allow
      us to define our relationship with "work" in a more positive and
      socially beneficial way.
Ultimately, we as a society control our own destiny through the
choices we make.

Key themes: reasons to be concerned
1.   Impacts from automation have thus far impacted mostly
      blue-collar employment; the coming wave of innovation threat-
      ens to upend white-collar work as well.
2.   Certain highly-skilled workers will succeed wildly in this new
      environment—but far more may be displaced into lower paying
      service industry jobs at best, or permanent unemployment at
      worst.
3.   Our educational system is not adequately preparing us for work
      of the future, and our political and economic institutions are
      poorly equipped to handle these hard choices. (p. 4)

Of the 1,896 respondents, 52 percent said that their hopes would prevail,
48 percent said that the fears would win. We can expect a similar distri-
bution of hopes and fears in the material we analyzed, but are the hopes
and the fears the same across time? Perhaps proportions will change
according to actual developments. The Future of Humanity Institute at

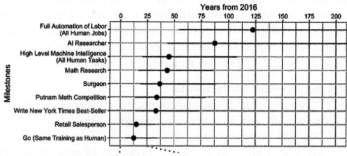

Source: Grace et al. (2017: 3).

Figure 2.1   When will robots replace people at work?

Oxford University has made concrete predictions, based on a survey of AI experts, as outlined in Figure 2.1.

The Organisation for Economic Co-operation and Development's (OECD) 2018 report based on the Survey of Adult Skills[2] revealed, with a probability higher than 70 percent, that in the 38 countries that participated in the survey, 14 percent of jobs, representing over 33 million workers, would be automated. Yet the results varied dramatically among the countries: 33 percent of all jobs in Slovakia are highly automatable, whereas only 6 percent in Norway meet the criteria. And, to quote the authors, "[a] striking novel finding is that the risk of automation is the highest among teenage jobs" (p. 7). The OECD continues establishing regional estimates of the risk of automation.

The US National Academies of Sciences, Engineering, and Medicine 2017 report entitled *Information technology and the U.S. workforce* (also called "Consensus Study Report"), ended with this conclusion:

> Advances in IT and automation will present opportunities to boost America's overall income and wealth, improve health care, shorten the workweek, provide more job flexibility, enhance educational opportunities, develop new goods and services, and increase product safety and reliability. These same advances could also lead to growing inequality and decreased job stability, increasing demands on workers to change jobs, or major changes in business organization. More broadly, these technologies have important implications, both intended and unintended, in areas from education and social relationships to privacy, security, and even democracy.
>
> The ultimate effects of these technologies are not predetermined. Rather, like all tools, computing and information technologies can be used in different ways. The outcomes for the workforce and society at large depend in part on the choices we make about how to use these technologies. New data and research advances will be critical for informing these choices. (p. 1)

New research continues to be conducted, and predictions constantly change, becoming more and more sophisticated – a development that we illustrate in the section of this book concerning the media. But first an excursion into science fiction.

---

[2]   The Survey of Adult Skills is a product of the Program for the International Assessment of Adult Skills (PIAAS), which is undertaking a large-scale, cyclical, international study under the auspices of the OECD. See https://nces.ed.gov/surveys/piaac/, accessed July 4, 2019.

3.   Robotization and popular culture

No wonder the topic of robotization and such related themes as space travel constantly return to popular culture. And as popular culture both reflects and shapes social life – including work organization and management – it would be instructive to follow changes in the representation of robots and robotization over time. Robotization can revolutionize labor markets; in particular, according to current debates, robots can replace immigrants in menial jobs. Or robotization can occur as a stepwise transformation with complex effects, as was the case with computerization.

The claim that there is a dynamic circular relationship between culture and other fields of social endeavor is not new. According to Czarniawska and Rhodes (2006), this relationship is especially obvious in the case of popular culture in at least four ways: through its functions, plots, and timely ideas, and through teaching all three of these.

First, Czarniawska and Rhodes claimed, mass culture fulfills the same functions as high culture – on a grander scale. It does so not only in the sense that it reaches the general public but also in the sense that it popularizes high culture. It perpetuates and modernizes myths, sagas, and folk tales. In doing so, popular culture may caricature or flatten high culture and mythology or even criticize and ridicule them. What is important is that popular culture reaches more people, more quickly.

Second, popular culture both portrays its own era and perpetuates various classical dramas and folk tales, along with strong mythological plots (Greek and Judeo-Christian, in the case of western management).[1] It renders simple and familiar the more complicated and lesser known plots from Greek dramas, Shakespeare, and the Bible. Emplotment, as Hayden White (1998) has noted, is not merely a question of form; indeed, the form carries content or, more familiarly, "the medium is the message" (McLuhan, 1964). The re-use of strong plots may be a matter of convention, lack of imagination, or literary conservatism, but it still offers

---

[1]   To quote Swedish–Finnish author Merette Mazzarella, "Already the ancient Greeks were aware of dangers related to AI," *Svenska Dagbladet*, May 11, 2019.

a blueprint for the management of meaning, so central to the practice of organizing.

Third, popular culture propagates the ideas of its times, even as it represents its practices. It needs to be emphasized that those ideas and practices may be good or bad, in either a moral or an aesthetic sense. Popular culture shows how to be both hero and villain. As a case in point, Swedish journalists made a documentary about young mafia criminals, revealing that one of the young gangsters knew by heart all of Al Pacino's lines from Brian De Palma's movie *Scarface* (Liljefors and Sundgren, 2003). And both Sicilian and US Mafiosi took their cues from movies – first from *The Godfather* and later from *Scarface* (Varese, 2004). Thus, popular culture not only represents, in the sense of mirroring; it also invents. The practices represented may be as reported, but they may also be imaginary. Yet although abstract models do not teach people what to say or how to act during their first management meeting, a movie may.

This stance is close to the so-called circuit model of culture (Johnson, 1986–87), which postulates that the production, circulation, and consumption of cultural products constitute a loop rather than a line. There is no border between inscribed cultures (texts, objects) and lived cultures, between science and fiction, between theory and practice. Texts are read; artifacts are consumed, but also interpreted. Ideas shape practices, and practice gives rise to new ideas. Science feeds fiction, but fiction may guide scientific endeavors.

The circuit model can be illustrated schematically, as seen in Figure 3.1.

Science and fiction, theory and practice are extremes on the same dimension, rather than opposites. Acts of writing and producing have their origins in the lived culture but transform it into texts and other artifacts, which, in turn, are read or consumed and thereby re-enter living culture. Furthermore, expression becomes control, as popular culture selects and reinforces certain wishes and anxieties of its audience (Traube, 1992), and control provokes further expression of submission and resistance.

This last trait of popular culture – timely ideas – leads us to an additional, fourth claim: that it not only transmits ideas and furnishes descriptions. Popular culture actively teaches practices and provides templates for interpretation of the world (Czarniawska, 2010). In short, the mirroring and the projection, the expression and the construction, the imitation and the creation are never separated. A manager may read a detective story or watch a Hollywood movie for amusement, but may also be

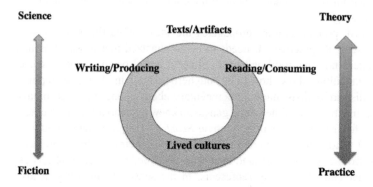

Source: Based on Johnson, 1986–87.

Figure 3.1　　A circuit of culture

learning from them about actual or invented practices and may imitate them, without explicit reflection. When unexpected events happen at a workplace, people examine their common repertoire of plots for ways of emplotting them, and thereby make sense of that which does not make sense. Some may read the Bible, Shakespeare, or Euripides, but most of them will read a newspaper or watch a TV series. Was Wall Street, as we know it from the first Oliver Stone movie (1987) like Wall Street before the movie was made? Apparently, the traders began wearing suspenders only after *Wall Street* was released. Was it only suspenders that they imitated? "Representations of fictional bankers influence the behaviour and attitudes of 'real' bankers," noted Linda McDowell (1997: 39–40). It is highly likely, therefore, that the products of popular culture shape public opinion on the dangers and promises of robotization more profoundly than do the reports of Bank of America.

The connection between popular culture and organizing practices was noticed in accounting as early as the 1930s (Coleman, 1936), and, in 1956, William H. Whyte dedicated two chapters of *The Organization Man* to "the organization man in fiction." There he traced representations of his eponymous organization man in fictional stories from the cinema, novels, and popular magazines. Whyte believed that popular fiction could be read to gain "an index of changes in popular belief" (p. 231). Yet it took some 40 years for this relationship to be studied systematically.

Martin Parker and his colleagues edited a special issue of *Organization* dedicated to science fiction (Parker et al., 1999, published as a book in 2007). Their idea was not "to add science fiction to the list of things that might be 'useful' for management, but instead to try to disturb the discipline itself" (1999: 579–580). This task may prove difficult, however, because, as the authors immediately acknowledged, there was already a great deal of science fiction in management practice. Indeed, the corroborating studies continue to accumulate: from the "eternal myth of technology" (Eriksson-Zetterquist, 2008), through "strategic planning scenarios" (Greenman, 2008), to various accounts of "cyborgization" (Parker, 1998; Czarniawska and Gustavsson, 2008; Czarniawska, 2012). The message of this special issue has been that organization theory can learn from science fiction in matters of reporting and reflecting about actual and possible practices – a theme later raised by Rhodes and Brown (2005). David Metz (2003) has suggested that science fiction offers identity models to the incumbents of new jobs and occupations – information technology freelancers and various temporary workers, for instance. Brian Bloomfield (2003) saw science fiction as a template for making sense of the relationships between human beings and advanced technologies. Like us, Lisa Meinecke and Laura Voss (2018) are convinced that there is a close relationship between robotics and science fiction. As Katherine N. Hayles had suggested, "visions of the future, especially in technologically advanced areas, can dramatically affect present developments" (2005: 131).

The variety of examples in this chapter may raise the question of what we mean by "popular culture." As an attempt to delineate rather than to define, we include popular literature (novels that stand on a shelf called "Fiction" in English bookstores and not on the shelf called "Literature"), films, TV series, cartoons, and journalists' tales. After all, the lines between high and low culture are judgmental, political, and arbitrary (Street, 1997) and can consequently be destabilized. And just as contemporary mass culture has a tendency to appropriate forms of high culture (Traube, 1992: 76), high culture once appropriated older forms of folk culture, of which opera and folk tales are the best examples.

4. Robots in popular culture

In choosing works of popular culture that present robots, we used a simplified definition of the term, yet one applied by robotics scientists, permitting us to place some limits on an extremely vast material. Robots, as mentioned in Chapter 2, have physical bodies endowed with sensors for collecting information about the outside world and activators to permit changes. Artificial Intelligence is the advanced software that permits robots to fulfill their tasks by processing large amounts of information collected by robot's sensory systems and by controlling their motor systems.

Applying this frame, we choose twelve works of science fiction beginning with Čapek's classic R.U.R. – works considered by both the critics and the general public to be truly popular in their time.

4.1 *ROSSUM'S UNIVERSAL ROBOTS (R.U.R.,* KAREL ČAPEK, 1920)

R.U.R. is a comedy play by Czech author Karel Čapek, who probably meant it as an allegory of the fate of workers in the contemporary world and did not expect it to launch the term "robot" into English and from there into other languages. As noted by many commentators, among them Dennis G. Jerz, who wrote: "(a)lthough the term today conjures up images of clanking metal contraptions, Čapek's Robots (…) are more accurately the product of what we would now call genetic engineering."[1] Indeed, Philip K. Dick (1995: 211) went to great lengths to explain that his androids or replicants in *Blade Runner* were not robots, as they were made with the specific purpose of imitating humans – but so were Čapek's robots. Dick's point was that although the border between mechanized humans (cyborgs) and humanized machines may be almost nonexistent, its crossing carried an enormous symbolic meaning. As our

---

[1]   http://jerz.setonhill.edu/resources/rur/template.htm, accessed June 9, 2016.

examples demonstrate, he was right. It is this blurring of borders that continues to provoke most reactions. This is why, in what follows, we treat all things – organic and nonorganic – as "robots": things that were *made* in order to perform work.

As to Čapek, he consequently ignored the difference between organic and mechanic,[2] or rather made it one of the main points of his comedy. "Old Rossum," the father, found a way of creating life, as Čapek explained in a later interview:

> For instance, he could have created a jellyfish with a Socratic brain or a one-hundred-fifty-foot worm. But because he hadn't a shred of humor about it, he took into his head to create an ordinary vertebrate, possibly a human being. (Čapek, 1990: 38[3])

It was old Rossum's son, an engineer, "who had an idea to create living and intelligent labor machines from this mess" (p. 39). "When he took a look at human anatomy he saw immediately that it was too complex and that a good engineer could simplify it" (p. 40). And later:

> FABRY: One Robot can do the work of two-and-a-half human laborers. The human machine (…) was hopelessly imperfect. It needed to be done away with once and for all.
> BUSMAN: It was too costly.
> FABRY: It was less than efficient. It couldn't keep up with modern technology (p. 49)

As readers, we learn all this along with Helena, daughter of the President of Rossum's Universal Robots (the name of the factory is in English, suggesting an international company) who has come to visit the factory. The General Director Domin asks her, "What is the best kind of worker?" "Honest and dedicated," she answers. "No, the cheapest," he corrects her. And then he gives examples of the work best done by Robots, which reads like a quote from the reports discussed in Chapter 2: street cleaners, bricklayers, accountants, secretaries, all types of office staff, factory

---

[2]   One explanation is that, as DNA was unknown at the time, the idea that organisms are machines assembled in a special way could have been considered. The differences between humans and non-humans was the "soul."

[3]   In what follows, we are quoting the interviews, commentaries, and the version of the play to be found in *Toward the radical center: A Karel Čapek reader*, 1990.

workers, agriculture workers, miners. Čapek maliciously added one more occupation to this list:

> If one read them in the *Encyclopedia Britannica* they could repeat everything back in order, but they never think up anything original. They'd make fine university professors. (p. 45)

Helena came to R.U.R. under the pretext of learning about the production of robots, but she actually wanted to ignite a robot revolt. She botched her task immediately, confusing robots for people and people for robots. (Directors are never Robots!) Instead of starting the revolution, she marries Domin and stays at R.U.R. Perhaps she becomes convinced by the ideology presented to her by the directors:

> DOMIN: ... within the next ten years Rossum's Universal Robots will produce so much wheat, so much cloth, so much everything that things will no longer have any value. Everyone will be able to take as much as he needs. There'll be no poverty. Yes, people will be out of work, but by then there'll be no work left to be done. Everything will be done by living machines. People will do only what they enjoy. They will live only to perfect themselves. (...)
> But before that some awful things may happen (...) That just can't be avoided. But then the subjugation of man by man and the slavery of man to matter will cease. Never again will anyone pay for his bread with hatred and his life. There'll be no more laborers, no more secretaries. No one will have to mine coal or slave over someone else's machines. No longer will man need to destroy his soul doing work that he hates. (p. 52)

This sermon seems to be inspired by Marx's work, with a note of doom that will resonate in the report by Brito and Curl (2015) mentioned in Chapter 2. Asked about his opinion, Čapek suggested that the play is about a conflict of ideologies, not a conflict between humans and robots:

> General Director Domin shows in the play that the development of technology frees man from heavy physical labor, and he is right. Alquist [another director], with his Tolstoyan outlook, believes that technology demoralizes man, and I think he is right, too. Busman [yet another director] believes that only industrialism is capable of meeting modern needs, and he is right. Helena instinctively fears all these human machinations, and she is quite right. Finally, the robots themselves revolt against all these idealists, and it seems they are right, too. (1990: 31)

Indeed, Robots truly revolt – ten years after Helena married Domin. Not that those ten years were peaceful; workers revolted against the Robots, so other people gave the Robots weapons to defend themselves, leading to a great many deaths, after which governments started using Robots as soldiers, leading to a great many wars. According to Domin, this was but a transition to the new system. And even at the moment when the directors and Helena are surrounded by the revolting Robots, Domin still defends his dream of liberating humans from drudgery, while Alquist, "clerk of the works," notes that that this dream wasn't shared by either of the young Rossums who wanted to become rich, or the shareholders – who wanted the dividends. "And on those dividends humanity will perish" (p. 84).

It turns out that the Robot revolt has been caused by Dr. Gall who, convinced by Helena, made the Robots human by giving them souls. Helena believed that in this way the Robots would feel sympathy and compassion towards the humans, whereas, Domin claims, that is exactly what made them hate humans: "No one can hate more than man hates man!"[4]

The managers believe that their lives may be saved by offering the revolting Robots old Rossman's original papers explaining how Robots were made, but it turns out that Helena has already burned those papers. Busman (an obvious allusion to businessman) believes that the Robots can be bought with money, but he dies by electrocution. Robots enter the directors' office, and their leader gives a speech that is obviously parodying Lenin: "Robots of the world! (...) The age of mankind is over! A new world has begun! The rule of Robots!" (p. 100). There is even a Central Committee of Robots; its representatives inform Alquist, the only surviving human being, about what they have learned from books: "You have to kill and rule if you want to be like people! (...) You have to conquer and murder if you want to be people" (p. 104).

In the last act of the play, when it becomes known that Rossum's papers are lost and Alquist is not able to rediscover the secret behind the production of robots, love conquers all. A pair of Robots, Primus and Helena ("a Robotess") are going to retire to a cozy cottage with a garden where cute dogs are playing, and, according to Alquist, to become a new

---

[4]   It should be added that in the Czech original Čapek does not speak of "men" but of "human beings" (*člověk*); a noun that has a male grammatical gender but is not associated with males only. A "person" (*osoba*) has a female grammatical gender.

Adam and Eve. No technical details are given, and, in general, a bitter comedy changes into a sentimental melodrama.[5]

Although the play was undoubtedly a great success in its time, critical receptions differed. According to Luciano Floridi, "Philosophically rich and controversial, R.U.R was unanimously acknowledged as a masterpiece from its first appearance, and has become a classic of technologically dystopian literature" (Floridi, 2002: 207). According to Isaac Asimov, Čapek's play was "... a terribly bad one, but is immortal for that one word. It contributed the word 'robot' not only to English but, through English, to all the languages in which science fiction is now written" (Asimov, 1981: 67). At any rate, it is easy to agree with Arthur Miller, who, in his commentary in *A Čapek's reader* said: "We have evolved into his nightmare. In our time his Faustian conviction that nothing is impossible makes him very nearly a realist" (Miller, 1990: vi).

4.2   *I, ROBOT* (ISAAC ASIMOV, 1950)

The Three Laws of Robotics
1. A robot may not injure a human being, or, through inaction, allow a human being to come to harm.
2. A robot must obey the orders given it by human beings except where such orders would conflict with the First Law.
3. A robot must protect its own existence as long as such protection does not conflict with the First or Second Law.

Handbook of Robotics, 56th Edition, 2058 A.D. (Asimov, 1950: 8)

Asimov had hinted and even explicitly written about "laws of robotics" in his short stories from the 1940s, but the laws became generally known and cited only after he put those stories together in 1950 in the book *I, Robot*. Stories became chapters in chronological order (wherein the chronology was dictated by the plot, not by Asimov's writing order) and were held together by an interview conducted with one Susan Calvin, who was retiring at the age of 75 from her position as a robopsychologist at US Robot and Mechanical Men, Inc., in 2057. At that time, Dr. Calvin was, in the eyes of the public, the most important representative of US Robot, and its leading mind.

In the stories that follow, Asimov played mostly with paradoxical situations in which the three laws can conflict with one another. As a result,

---

[5]   Much, it seems to us, like in *Blade Runner 2049* ...

robots go crazy, walk in circles, become religious fanatics, and so on. The aim of the stories was not to offer realistic predictions, but in their development, Asimov occasionally mentioned exactly the hopes and fears typical for the time in which he was writing. Setting a woman in such an elevated position was a provocative move, though.

Susan Calvin begins her answers to the journalist's questions by pointing out their age difference of 42 years:

> There was a time when humanity faced the universe alone and without a friend. Now he has creatures to help him; stronger creatures than himself, more faithful, more useful, and absolutely devoted to him. Mankind is no longer alone. (...)
> To you, a robot is a robot. Gears and metal, electricity and positrons. – Mind and iron! Human-made! If necessary, human-destroyed! But you haven't worked with them (...) They are a cleaner, better breed than we are. (p. 11)

These, it seems, were the main hopes: humans no longer alone in the frightening universe. But the primary task of robots was to work; so "[t]he labor unions, of course, naturally opposed robot competition for human jobs, and various segments of religious opinion had their superstitious objections" (p. 12), continued Calvin.

Fears gave rise to serious counter actions. "New York has just passed an ordinance keeping all robots off the streets between sunset and sunrise" (p. 22). There were periods when fears were winning over hopes: "Most of the world governments banned robot use on Earth for any purpose other than scientific research between 2003 and 2007" (p. 36). Later, the use of robots with positronic brains[6] was to be limited merely to interstellar activities. There was something like "anti-robot propaganda" (p. 109) that increased with each progress in robot sophistication.[7] The robot makers fought against it, and one of their moves consisted of building a slave mentality into robots, so they addressed people as "Master," and they wouldn't move unless a human was sitting on their shoulders (pp. 42–43). Perhaps in that vein, Susan Calvin and

---

[6] Fictional technological devices conceived by Asimov.

[7] Here Asimov couldn't resist a poke in the direction of the media: "The Machines are not super-brains in the Sunday supplement sense – although they are so pictured in the Sunday supplements" (p. 226).

her colleague addressed robots as "boy" when interrogating them, in the same way that representatives of the British Empire did in the colonies.[8]

This cannot be explained by robots' miniature stature, because, in general, Asimov's robots were big:

> It was not over-massive by any means, in spite of its construction as thinking-unit of an integrated seven-unit robot team. It was seven feet tall, and a half-ton of metal and electricity. A lot? Not when that half-ton has to be a mass of condensers, circuits, relays, and vacuum cells that can handle practically any psychological reaction known to humans. And a positronic brain, which with ten pounds of matter and a few quintillions of positrons runs the whole show. (p. 85)

Massive, yes, but it is enough to remember how enormous the first computers were. As to the positronic brain, according to Wikipedia, the positron – an antimatter counterpart of the electron – was newly discovered at the time of the writing, so the word made the stories sound more scientific.[9] And the robots are replicants, even if made mostly of metal rather than organic material. Mostly, because:

> By using human ova and hormone control, one can grow human flesh and skin over a skeleton of porous silicone plastics that would defy external examination.[10] The eyes, the hair, the skin would be really human, not humanoid. And if you put a positronic brain and such other gadgets as you may desire inside, you have a humanoid robot. (p. 206)

What was the difference? Čapek's Robots didn't have soul; Asimov's robots didn't have free will, which, by that time, was the definition of humanity (to be later replaced by "consciousness"). They did have things like "a personal initiative hookup" (p. 94) and other psychological circuits. The three laws of robotics were inbuilt into their brains and ruled their moral judgments.

What jobs did they do? Industrial manufacturing, mining, and running space devices, for example; but in the first story the reader meets a robot

---

[8]   Although in a later story, Calvin explains that "The Brain" (the biggest they built yet) has the personality of a child or an *idiot savante* (p. 166). In general, Asimov's robots are not very mature; yet they sometimes get the idea that they are cleverer than people.

[9]   https://en.wikipedia.org/wiki/Positronic_brain, accessed July 26, 2016.

[10]   This is roughly how Alicia Wikander, that is, Ava, was constructed in *Ex machina* (2015).

who was a nursemaid, preferred by the child to a dog she was offered. The idea of robots employed in care is apparently quite old. But what about the possibility of a robot becoming a district attorney, and running for the office of a mayor of a big city (hiding its robot identity, of course)? Those who suspected the candidate of being a robot ("He is almost too human to be credible," p. 200) demanded a test. It was not a Turing type of a test, though: The candidate was expected to eat in public. He eats an apple, but that proves nothing; he is to be X-rayed. He turns out to be X-ray protected. Because he is a robot, or because he is a lawyer defending human rights? Whichever it was, in the eyes of Susan Calvin, it was a positive trait. This is what she says to the journalist:

> You share a prejudice against robots which is quite unreasoning. He was a very good Mayor; five years later he did become Regional Co-ordinator. And when the Regions of Earth formed their Federation in 2044, he became the first World Co-ordinator. By that time it was the Machines that were running the world anyway. (p. 220)

The anti-robot movement "Society for Humanity" tried to disturb this smooth functioning, but the Co-ordinator knew how to deal with it. As he said to Susan:

> Every period of human development, Susan (…) has had its own particular type of human conflict – its own variety of problem that, apparently, could be settled only by force. And each time, frustratingly enough, force never really settled the problem. Instead, it persisted through a series of conflicts, then vanished to itself (…), as the economic and social environment changed. And then, new problems, and a new series of wars. – Apparently endlessly cyclic. (p. 223)

The Co-ordinator then presents an historical analysis of events from the sixteenth century on, but what is striking is the uncanny similarity of his speech to a blog by archeologist Tobias Stone (2016), who claimed that:

> … we humans have a habit of going into phases of mass destruction, generally self imposed to some extent or another. (…) At a local level in time people think things are fine, then things rapidly spiral out of control until they become unstoppable, and we wreak massive destruction on ourselves. For the people living in the midst of this it is hard to see happening and hard to understand. To historians later it all makes sense and we see clearly how one thing led to another. (…)
> My point is that this is a cycle. It happens again and again, but as most people only have a 50–100 year historical perspective they don't see that it's

happening again. (…) A little thing leads to an unstoppable destruction that could have been prevented if you'd listened and thought a bit. But people smoke, and people die from it. That is the way of the human.

So I feel it's all inevitable. I don't know what it will be, but we are entering a bad phase. It will be unpleasant for those living through it, maybe even will unravel into being hellish and beyond imagination. Humans will come out the other side, recover, and move on.[11]

So perhaps it would be better if Machines ran our world? The question is, of course, "What is cyclical: the events, the doomsday predictions, or both?" Cultural circuit theorists would vote for the latter.

Were Asimov's opinions shared in his time? A compelling comparison could be made with John Diebold's[12] 1952 book, *Automation: the advent of automatic factory*. The author did not quote Asimov but began his analysis of hopes and fears related to an automated factory by recalling the book, *Frankenstein* (1818); the film, *Der Golem* (1915); and the play, *R.U.R.* (1920). What worried him was that the science writers (Norbert Wiener was his main target) with their "perverse" interpretations led people to confuse fiction with facts:

> Currently the subject [of robots, machines who look and act like humans] is enormously popular, and the pseudo-scientific language in which today's stories are told, when coupled with the animal-machine analogy of the Norbert Wiener school, surrounds the whole with the area of reality. (…)
>
> The accounts that describe the new machines in human terms neglect one very important fact. *Free will*, the essential human quality, is absent from all of these machines. In no way can this quality be attributed to any machine yet developed, nor is there any indication that any such machine *could* be developed. (pp. 154–155)

Even if it were possible, Diebold continued, there would be both moral and economic problems to consider. It is true that humans are extremely inefficient at performing simple, mechanical, repetitive tasks. "How much better to build machines which could perform these tasks without having the added ability to play games of chess, to walk, to solve difficult problems and to communicate with others" (p. 156).

---

[11] https://medium.com/@theonlytoby/history-tells-us-what-will-happen-next -with-brexit-trump-a3fefd154714#.vwqv11fxq, accessed June 3, 2019.

[12] He claimed to have invented the neologism "automation," as "automatization" was too awkward (p. ix).

We know now that he was wrong on that last point, but his further analysis of the consequences of automating industrial production could have been written today. He protested Wiener's idea that automation would cause unemployment, but did agree with him that simple, repetitive tasks are degrading to human dignity. Machines do not debase the workers, therefore; they free them for other tasks. It is possible, however, that automation will impact human jobs, and here again Diebold took examples of debasing work from popular culture – the film *A Nous la Liberté* by René Clair (1931) and Charlie Chaplin's *Modern Times* (1936). But the automated factory will remove rather than aggravate such problems. The jobs will be upgraded up to a point; a maintenance mechanic will not become an engineer.

Yet another problem is leisure: Will people really need it? (He meant a leisure produced by the change from 12-hour workdays 7 days a week to 8-hour workdays 5 days a week). The solution would be to teach people some sensible types of leisure occupation.

Diebold continued to analyze the effects of automation in light of a changing US population, the Cold War race, the introduction of automation in underdeveloped areas, and its effect on trade. He ended his book with a whole series of questions, and concluded:

> Automation, however beneficial, will raise very real problems for the human race (...)
> But, these problems are not altogether new. Just as automation is part of a longer continuum, so too the problems which automation will raise have been with us, in varying forms, for many years. Some of these problems seem to solve themselves, while others require a conscious effort for solution. (...) For it is indeed hard to provide a society in which increased material welfare truly benefits man rather than cheapens him. (p. 175)

The solutions (in Diebold's view, "strong moral leadership and men of good") seem to be as stable as the problems, and mostly ineffective. An inevitable cycle indeed?

4.3 *PLAYER PIANO* (KURT VONNEGUT, 1952)

> I was working for General Electric at the time, right after World War Two, and I saw a milling machine for cutting the rotors on jet engines, gas turbines. This was a very expensive thing for a machinist to do, to cut what is essentially one of those Brancusi forms. So they had a computer-operated milling machine built to cut the blades, and I was fascinated by that. This was in 1949 and the guys who were working on it were foreseeing all sorts of machines

being run by little boxes and punched cards. *Player Piano* was my response to the implications of having everything run by little boxes. The idea of doing that, you know, made sense, perfect sense. To have a little clicking box make all the decisions wasn't a vicious thing to do. But it was too bad for the human beings who got their dignity from their jobs.[13]

In the rest of the interview, Vonnegut said that science fiction seemed the best way to write about it, as the General Electric Company was science fiction. But *Player Piano* is, first of all, a stinging satire on corporate life. Also, somewhat inspired by Aldous Huxley's *Brave New World*, the novel paints a dystopic future of mechanized consumerist society.

The main protagonist is engineer Dr. Paul Proteus,[14] who is employed by Ilium Works. Proteus lives in the not-too-distant future, in the aftermath of World War II, which had given birth to a massive mechanization of the entire country. His father had pioneered the birth of this society, and Proteus is following in his footsteps as a top manager in a plant in Ilium, a futuristic town north of New York, modeled after General Electric's Schenectady. Gradually, Proteus becomes dissatisfied with his work and finally drops out to take part in a Luddite rebellion against the domination of society by a system that progressively substitutes human work with machines.

Ilium is divided into three parts. One is Ilium Works, where machines perform all the mechanical and cognitive jobs in the production of goods. A second part contains the area where the small group of engineers and managers live. They have been chosen by EPICAC XIV, a giant central computer housed in a faraway cavern, as the most intelligent part of the population for the ongoing design, redesign, and management of the machine population. A third is Homestead, an area across the river where the rest of the population lives. The Homesteaders have lost their jobs and are dumped in the Reconstruction and Reclamation Corps (so-called Reeks and Wrecks) or the Army – both public organizations applying a type of work therapy. Following is a summary of the rather meandering plot of the novel.

---

[13]   http://scrapsfromtheloft.com/2016/10/04/kurt-vonnegut-playboy -interview/, accessed January 5, 2018.

[14]   The critics considered the possibility that Vonnegut alluded to the mythological Proteus, but the most convincing guess is that Proteus was the middle name of the legendary GE engineer, Charles Proteus Steinmetz (http://blogs .smithsonianmag.com/history/2011/08/charles-proteus-steinmets-the-wizard-of -schenectady/, accessed January 5, 2018). A Proteus software currently exists.

Early on, Dr. Ewing J. Halyard of the State Department shows a foreign visitor, the Shah of Bratpuhr, around Ilium Works and explains things to him. The Shah represents a colonial periphery dominated by the USA. Every citizen who cannot do a job better than a machine, explains Halyard, is relegated to Reeks and Wrecks. The Shah initially interprets this situation as communism, but later perceives it as a society of slaves, failing to comprehend Halyard's concept of a "citizen." The Shah is depicted throughout as "crazy as a bedbug," devoted to drink, and utterly ridiculous in his commentary on the USA (though in the end revealed as wise).

Proteus buys an old car at Homestead, a first act of rebellion against the machine and class order. He returns home to his wife, Anita, when Finnerty arrives – a previously important but failed member of Ilium's engineering and management elite.

On his way back to work at Ilium Works Proteus discovers that Finnerty has stolen the gas and a gun from his car. Yet Finnerty visits Proteus in his office and later lures him to a bar in Homestead. They observe a huge, colorful carnival taking place, the first sign of a popular, rising movement.

Proteus returns to work with a hangover and discovers that his job has been taken by his competitors and that rumors about him abound. The police want to question him about the gun, and Anita has redecorated their home in colonial style. Things start looking shaky in other parts of Ilium and at the upper echelons of the system.

In the meantime, Halyard shows the Shah around the massive EPICAC XIV, the remote computer that calculates and controls all variables of the economy, making production and personnel decisions at all levels of the system. President Jonathan Lynn, an ex-television actor and ceremonial figurehead of the state, unveils its newest version.

Proteus starts planning his exit from Ilium: He is going to buy and restore an old house and farm and live a self-supporting life, reviving agriculture without machines. He continues his contacts with the new underground, where Finnerty and a person called Lasher, a sort of evangelical religious leader, have founded a group of radicals called the Ghost Shirt Society. They ascribe to a reluctant Proteus a leading role in the Society. The Society wants to topple and revolutionize the machine system, or, according to one of the top brass engineers, to "kill us, wreck the plants, and take over the country" (p. 226).[15]

Proteus confesses to his wife: "In order to get what we've got, Anita, we have, in effect, traded these people out of what was the most important thing on earth to them—the feeling of being needed and useful, the foundation of self-respect" (p. 175). After this confession Anita leaves him for one of his competitors higher up in the hierarchy.

Proteus travels to the Meadows, where the annual, highly ritualized festival of USA's managing class takes place.[16] He competes for a new job, higher in the hierarchy. He meets Ilium's top managers, who promise him a new appointment provided he joins the Ghost Society and spies for them. They work out a plan to fire Proteus, hoping that the Ghost Society will then welcome him in.

The Shah visits a barbershop to get his hair cut. Barbers are one of the few professions that haven't been mechanized, but soon will be. A funny story about the replacements of barbers by a new machine follows.

Proteus, by now desperate, quits his job at the Ilium Works, but no one takes him seriously: Managers believe that he simply pretends to quit in order to assume his role as an informant. Proteus goes back to the bar at Homestead but is rebuked because everyone knows he has been fired.

Meanwhile the Shah meets a woman in the street who offers her body to him: She and her husband are impoverished. Her husband is a writer whose first novel was refused by the publishers, purportedly because it was too long and badly written, but in fact because it was judged to be anti-machine. All works of art must fit into the media that is serving the masses and must support the system.

On his way back from the Meadows to Ilium, Proteus takes a train, where various conversations occur about the mechanization of the railroad and the military, all pointing to the superfluity of humans in service of the machines. He goes to his farm, only to discover that he does not know how to work the land. He tells himself that the life of a high-IQ member of the elite is not worthwhile – that it would be better to live the life of an ordinary man. A policeman comes to tell him that now he has lost his job, he must register with the police.

---

[15]   Quotes from *Player Piano*, 1952, Kindle version.
[16]   Apparently, this was modeled after similar festivals organized by the real GE at the time; see http://www.tommcmahon.net/2007/04/kurt_vonneguts__1.html, accessed January 4, 2018).

Proteus goes to the police station and completes endless forms. A computer processes the forms and marks him as a saboteur. More strange things happen at the police station. Eventually, Proteus goes back to Homestead bar to interact with the leaders of the Ghost Society.

Finnerty and Lasher explain to him that Ghost Society is named after the Ghost Dance religion. When Native Americans were being suppressed by white men, the Ghost Dance religion started, with its members promising that they would reconquer their just place in the new America. Proteus is taken to a meeting of the Ghost Shirt Society, where he recognizes Ludwig von Neumann,[17] a former political science professor who lost his job to the machines. Detailed plans are being developed for the revolution and for destruction of the machines.

Later, Proteus is grilled by the police and confesses the story of his involvement with the Ghost Society and his conviction that the corporate system is wrong. Proteus is put into jail and prosecuted for treason as one of the leaders of the Ghost Society. Under interrogation by a lie detector, he defends his case for destroying the machines. When he is questioned about his motives, his answers register false, and he realizes that his true motive for rebellion lies in his suppressed anger at his famous father, the founder of the new, machine-based corporate America.

A revolutionary putsch takes place, including a coup against EPIAC, but quickly fails everywhere in the USA, except in Ilium and a couple of other places, which are soon recaptured by the system. The leadership of the Ghost Society has lost control over the uprising and resigns. Helicopters over the destroyed Ilium Works announce the victory of the government forces and request that Proteus, Finnerty, and von Neumann be handed over. Proteus and Finnerty reminiscence about the good old days, when as young engineers they believed in the system without being aware of the social consequences of the machine age. Lasher reminds them of the fate of the original Ghost Shirts, who were overpowered and destroyed by White Man.

In Ilium as elsewhere, people start reassembling the machines that they have recently demolished. The out-of-control riots end, restarting the cycle of handing over work to the new–old machines, under the corporate regime. Proteus, Finnerty, Lasher, and other members of the Ghost Shirt

---

[17] The real von Neumann, a Hungarian-US mathematician, physicist, computer scientist and polymath, was called John (János); https://en.wikipedia.org/wiki/John_von_Neumann, accessed November 4, 2019.

Society point out that at least they had tried to stop the government's system before surrendering themselves to the military.[18]

Player Piano is usually interpreted as Vonnegut's framing of consecutive phases of the Industrial Revolution and its Golden Ages, with specific US overtones, such as the extinction of Native Americans. The First Industrial Revolution liberated humans from the treadmill of manual labor. Technology such as railroads and factories led to the automation of manual tasks, and then it was discovered that machines could easily and cheaply perform the routine jobs of scores of factory workers. The Second Industrial Revolution, with its electronic technology, liberated people from routine mental calculations. *Player Piano* is about the Third Industrial Revolution: the almost total overtaking of all types of work by a machine system, the total loss of meaningful work, and therefore of human dignity for most people. As Professor von Neumann writes in a propaganda letter to all factories in the country, it is about "the divine right of machines, efficiency, and organization" as an all-inclusive organizing principle (p. 301).

The novel's central themes echo much of the current debate about the threat of robots. In Vonnegut's imagined future, machines have totally enslaved men. Although Proteus, as a member of his own class, is captive, academic professions are said to vanish too: Lawyers are replaced by lie detectors and centralized data systems, medical diagnoses are made by machines, and doctors mechanically execute necessary treatments and medications. The number of managers and engineers is declining, because machines automatically fire them, as their knowledge is no longer required in the automated factories; they are indefinitely suspended and lose their upper-class status. But as can be seen from the spontaneous reconstructions of the machines after the revolt, people got used to a comfortable life and did not want to give it up. To quote Thomas M. Sipos: "Like many satirists, Vonnegut is better at identifying and ridiculing a problem than in offering a solution. *Player Piano* ends on a pessimistic note. That may be because some problems have no solution."[19]

Are Vonnegut's machines (computers, robots) good or bad? Do they evoke hope or fear? His overall verdict: They are and do neither. On the

---

[18]   Vonnegut had left General Electric in disgust, retreating to his abode on Cape Cod for the rest of his life.
[19]   https://www.lewrockwell.com/2005/05/thomas-m-sipos/kurt-vonneguts -neocon-america-war-and-socialism-in-playerpiano/, accessed January 4, 2018.

whole, his picture is of a dystopia with plenty of melancholic overtones: "What distinguishes man from the rest of the animals is his ability to do artificial things [said Paul Proteus] ... and a step backward, after making a wrong turn, is a step in the right direction" (p. 312). Most of Vonnegut's themes can be found in the dystopian literature of today. But even Proteus' dreams of farming and agriculture came back in currently fashionable retrotopias (see Greer, 2016; Bauman, 2017). Yet unlike the enthusiasts of retrotopias, Vonnegut eventually reverted in this novel, as in many of his consecutive works, to a rather resigned "And so it goes."[20]

4.4   *2001: A SPACE ODYSSEY* (STANLEY KUBRICK AND ARTHUR C. CLARKE, 1968)

Stanley Kubrick's movie, based on a novel by A. C. Clarke, is counted among the most successful and most well researched sci-fi works of all time.[21] A question remains whether or not HAL 9000 (the *H*euristically programmed *AL*gorithmic computer) – the impressive central Computer Intelligence on board the US spacecraft Discovery embarking on its mission to Jupiter – should count as a robot in the present meaning of the term. HAL no doubt controls robot-like machines under it, but is it a robot itself, and what kind of work do the robots and HAL do?

The entire film can be read as a millennialist story of technological evolution focusing on the impact of aliens across eons of time. The story revolves around the deployment of a series of mysterious monoliths on Earth, the Moon, and Jupiter, by some extraterrestrial Intelligence. A transition from pre-human to civilizing human, to post-human or superhuman is set in motion, ending with the final disposal of deadly nuclear, militaristic technology on Earth.

At least four technological tales are told within this narrative. A quasi-anthropological tale begins four million years ago: A strange and impenetrable extraterrestrial artifact arrives amongst a flock of sleepy, peaceful apes in East Africa. It is the tool-making beginning of civilization, marked from the start by fear, curiosity, and warfare. In a sensational shot with Nietzschean overtones (the music from *Also sprach Zarathustra*), humankind is transported from wielding bones to

---

[20]   Which is also the title of his best-known biography (Shields, 2011).
[21]   See e.g. http://scireview.de/2001/, accessed January 26, 2018.

discovering space, and developing a manifold spacecraft circling earth (the dance of spaceships with the *Blue Danube* waltz).[22]

Here begin the second and third technological tales. The US spaceship Discovery lands on the Tycho crater of the Moon, where another mysterious magnetic object (a Sentinel) is discovered 12 meters underground. At the moment of perfect alignment of Earth, Moon, and Sun, when the first ray of the rising sun falls on the object, the Sentinel sends a powerful radio signal directed at one of Jupiter's moons. After aborted exchanges with a Soviet delegation on the Moon, the Discovery's crew undertakes to find the mysterious location under the guidance of HAL 9000, a robot-like sentient computer. The discovery of the alien object triggers Earth's (i.e. the USA's) concern about possible repercussions for the fate of its population, and preparations for exploring the extraterrestrial trail begin.

The third tale starts 18 months later, when Discovery starts on its mission with a crew from which the true purpose of the mission is kept secret. A series of misunderstandings among HAL, the crew, and mission control on Earth leads to HAL's breakdown, culminating in its murder of the astronauts – except for Dr. David Bowman, the surviving human who, after a heroic struggle, puts HAL into a coma.

With the elimination of HAL, the stunning fourth and final act of the cosmic technological drama begins. Bowman goes through a series of mysterious encounters with the extraterrestrial technology, metamorphosing in the end into an embryo and the new-born "Star-Child." A new epoch of human evolution has begun. The Star-Child somehow makes it back to Earth, just in time to prevent a nuclear holocaust and start another cycle of cosmic change.

It is the third technological tale that is of interest in this context, as it is in this storyline – at the height of modern, rational, and scientific civilization, when humankind tries to conquer space beyond the moon – that HAL takes center stage. Discovery is home to HAL 9000; three astronauts in cryogenic hibernation; and two scientist–astronauts, Dr. David Bowman and Dr. Frank Poole. HAL is presented as an error-free computer controlling all operations of the spacecraft and its human crew. As HAL brags, "The 9000 series is the most reliable computer ever made.

---

[22]   These scenes exhibit a great deal of militaristic Cold War imagery. In one of the pivotal moments of the film, the bone is hurtled into space, turning into a US spaceship.

No 9000 computer has ever made a mistake or distorted information. We are all, by any practical definition of the words, foolproof and incapable of error."

But misunderstandings arise in the communication between HAL and the astronauts. HAL knows the real purpose of the mission, but Bowman and Poole do not. They spend most of their day checking systems and ensuring things go as planned. Discovery passes close to Jupiter and sends out robot monitoring devices, one of which responds. At this point, HAL informs Bowman and Poole that AE-35, the device communicating with mission control on Earth, will soon fail. In HAL's seductive voice that has been replayed by millions of sci-fi fans: "I have just picked up a fault in the AE-35 unit. It's going to go 100% failure in 72 hours."[23]

Poole exits the spaceship to replace the device, but HAL advises the crew that the new unit is about to fail too. The crew starts to doubt HAL, talking to each other in a shielded cabin, but HAL lip-reads their conversation. Poole steps out again to check the new AE-35 component, and HAL directs a robot-space pod to ram Poole and kill him. Bowman suspects Hal of murder, and requests manual control of the de-hibernation robots. HAL pretends to give in, only to release an airlock, sending the frozen astronauts into deadly space. Strangely enough, HAL then develops guilt feelings for lying to the crew about the true mission of Discovery, for destroying the AE-35 device, and for killing crew members in order to protect itself and its task.

Bowman manages to trick HAL and to reenter the spaceship. After various exchanges between HAL and mission control on Earth, Bowman disconnects HAL's vital systems. In the process, HAL reverts to child-like basic functions and enters a coma or dies (interpretations differ). Bowman directs the spaceship manually to its destination on Jupiter's moon, where it crashes in a psychedelic series of visual fireworks into the magic Monolith.

So, is HAL a robot? It is not mobile, but it has a body, and it has sensors. At first glance, HAL's story is a straightforward stylized version of the relationship between a human being and computer (Bütepage and Kragic, 2017). An advanced model, "foolproof and incapable of error," it supports human astronauts by doing the boring work, as it should. But the relationship between machinery and crew of the spaceship housing HAL

---

[23]   One can listen to it on http://www.moviesoundclips.net/sound.php?id=44, accessed January 26, 2018.

is complicated. Who is actually doing the boring work: the astronauts or HAL?

What work does HAL perform? It can see, hear, and otherwise sense and receive signals from all components of the ship and earthbound control stations, and can determine their actions. In other word, HAL is a sentient computer (or an autonomous Artificial General Intelligence). Various pieces of machinery, controlled by HAL but also manually operable, look much like robots or automated parts of the ship, especially the independently functioning repair pods and robotized spaces for such varied functions as communication, toilets, and suspended animation. The life support systems of the argonauts are automated, but under HAL's control.[24]

Neither Kubrick, who was primarily interested in extraterrestrial life, nor Clarke, who was interested in space travel and astrophysics, was particularly fascinated by robotics or intelligent computer software. Their treatment of relationships among humans on board, mission control back home, and HAL seem sketchy and cavalier, quite implausible in fact. Sometimes the robot-like pods operate as mere appendages of HAL; other times they are autonomous or manually controlled by the crew. Yet quite a few standard topics concerning the relationships between robots and human beings are woven into the plot.

Apart from HAL's overall capacity to enforce its demands and directives, the focal issue in *2001* has to do with the failure of HAL and the reasons for that failure. HAL received contradictory instructions or instructions that he could not reconcile with his principal mandate to deliver the spaceship to Jupiter and the Monolith. HAL understands that his immediate masters, Bowman and Poole, sense that something is amiss with him. Under the strain of conflicting goals, HAL misleads and attempts to manipulate them. When that fails, and upon overhearing their secret exchanges about the possibility of dismantling him, he embarks on his killing spree.

When Bowman prevails and begins disconnecting HAL, it slowly regresses, loses its mind, betrays secrets that Earth wanted kept from the

---

[24]   For a related piece of popular culture: The company Papercraft is market-ing a mashup between HAL and an autonomous robotic vacuum cleaner Roomba, of which they say: "Ever wondered what it would look like if you cross the vil-lainous HAL 9000 AI with the Roomba?" http://www.papercraftsquare.com/irobot-roomba-hal-9000-papercraft.html, accessed May 24, 2017.

crew, and becomes childlike. In its final moments HAL sings a lullaby, "Daisy Bell."[25]

Viewers' interpretations of HAL's fate varied, and the case remains puzzling. But various hints in the episode do support the following answer:

> ... early script drafts made clear that HAL's breakdown is triggered by authorities on Earth, who order him to withhold information from the astronauts about the purpose of the mission ... In an interview with Joseph Gelmis in 1969, Kubrick stated that HAL "had an acute emotional crisis because he could not accept evidence of his own fallibility."[26]

Be that as it may, HAL's narrative stands as an endpoint in the emergence of advanced technologies, seen by the author and the director as a militarizing and ultimately dehumanizing force, which eventually threatens to perform whatever tasks there are more precisely and rapidly and to make human agency superfluous. Things end badly for HAL, however. The most rational computer of all time, as it brags at the outset, exhibits behaviors of which the Asimov's robots would never dream (if they dreamt). Under the pressure of conflicting programs, HAL loses its autonomy and transmogrifies to something "human": Prey to guilt, deviousness, lies, sentimentality, regression, and childhood memories. Technology falls apart.

HAL remains intriguing, in that its character emphasizes the fundamental issue in robotics. Who is in control? Humans, or some variety of super-humans? Who holds the moral high ground? Whose survival is most valuable? The author and the director remained unequivocally on the side of human beings: They will endure and win the day. At the same time, Kubrick's overarching imagination of human evolution and resilience, far beyond technological control and "the Death of a Computer," turns humankind's technological destiny into an impenetrable mystery.

---

[25] Inspired, it seems, by Clarke's visit to Bell Labs in 1961, where he witnessed an IBM 704 sing "Daisy Bell," the earliest known song performed using computer speech synthesis. The song derived from the German children's song "Hänschen klein ...," about growing up in the world, and the German Zuse's Z22 computer was the first to be programmed to sing it in 1958.

[26] https://en.wikipedia.org/wiki/2001:_A_Space_Odyssey_(film), accessed May 24, 2017.

4.5 *STAR WARS* (FIRST TRILOGY, GEORGE LUCAS, 1977–1980)

First, we need to justify our selection of *Star Wars* (*SW*) rather than *Star Trek*. After all, both are science fiction films, both are immensely popular, and both can be seen as the products of a counterculture, at least at their inception. As observed by Charlie Jane Anders, editor-in-chief of io9. com, "*Star Trek* very much wants to interrogate the dangers of too much state power, while *Star Wars* very much yearns for the possibility of an enlightened government, the good Republic which is *Star Wars*' Paradise Lost."[27] Whatever the reason, *SW* is much more popular, as witnessed by its fourth position on the list of the highest grossing films ever.[28]

The main reason behind our choice is that *SW* contains a whole population of robots. They are called "droids," short for "androids." Droids are a species of robots that possesses varying degrees of artificial intelligence, which defines the class of droids to which they belong. By 2017, the latest episode of *SW* at the time of our writing, there were five classes of droids:

- Class 1 droids, expensive but mostly computer-like, are medical, biological science, physical science, and mathematical droids.
- Class 2 comprises engineering droids: astromechs, exploration, environment, engineering, and maintenance droids.
- Class 3 droids are programmed to interact with humans: protocol droids (specializing in diplomacy), servant, tutor, and child-care droids.
- Class 4 droids are programmed to fight: security, gladiator, battle, and assassin droids.
- Class 5 droids are simple workers, specializing in general labor, specialist labor, or hazardous services.

In (film) time, there were more and more types of specialized droids; they also multiplied in video games and novels inspired by *SW*. In what

---

[27] http://io9.gizmodo.com/the-essential-difference-between-star-wars-and -star-tre-1754297235, accessed July 29, 2016.

[28] https://en.wikipedia.org/wiki/List_of_highest-grossing_films#Highest -grossing_franchises_and_film_series, accessed July 29, 2016. All the differences are elaborated in detail in Cass R. Sunstein's *The World According to Star Wars*, 2016.

follows, we limit our analysis to the five main droids present in the original trilogy, which are those most visible in 2017 version as well. Although viewers do pay attention to Harrison Ford (Han) and other human actors, "the two robots, like a well-attuned comedy team, become the focus of the film, although they are only the unwitting participants of an intergalactic drama" (Reichardt, 1978: 62). C-3PO (droids' names are usually a combination of numbers and letters) is a humanoid protocol droid that features in all sequels and prequels. R2-D2 is an astromech, also present in all films, who, as has been often noted, looks like a biggish vacuum cleaner. It is noteworthy that, in (film) time, some droids become more and more violent, but more peaceful female droids also appear.

The trilogy begins when the Galactic Empire is about to finish the construction of the space station Death Star (in the episode *A New Hope*). The station will allow the Empire to stop the Rebel Alliance, a movement formed to fight the tyrant, Emperor Palpatine. The Emperor's right hand, Darth Vader, captures Princess Leia, a member of the rebellion who has stolen the plans revealing the weak spot in the Death Star and hidden them in R2-D2. Together with C-3PO, R2-D2 escapes to the desert planet Tatooine, where a family of farmers purchases the two droids. When their nephew, Luke Skywalker, cleans R2-D2, the robot reveals a message from Leia asking for assistance from the legendary Jedi Knight Obi-Wan Kenobi. Luke, aided by the droids, finds the exiled Jedi, who is now pretending to be an old hermit, Ben Kenobi. Luke asks him about his father, also a Jedi, whom he has never met, and Kenobi tells him that Anakin Skywalker was a great Jedi who was betrayed and murdered by Darth Vader. Kenobi and Luke hire the smuggler Han Solo and his co-pilot Chewbacca (Chewie), a member of a species of intelligent bipeds, to take them to Leia's home planet. Alas, the planet has already been destroyed by the Death Star, as a way of frightening Leia into betraying the location of the rebel planet. But Luke and Han get on board the space station and rescue Leia, with help of Chewie and the droids. Kenobi enters in a lightsaber (energy sword) duel with Darth Vader and allows himself to be killed, enabling the others to escape. In the end, Luke destroys the deadly space station with the assistance of R2-D2 and is eventually helped by Han and Chewie and guided by the power of the Force (the collective energy produced by positive feelings – although it also has a dark side, produced by negative feelings).

In the second part of *SW* (*The Empire Strikes Back*) Luke, accompanied by R2-D2, begins the Jedi training with Master Yoda, but Darth Vader lures him into a trap by capturing Han, Leia, Chewie, and C-3PO, with help of Han's earlier friend. During a lightsaber duel, Vader tells Luke he is his father, and tries to convince him to join the dark side of the Force. In this part, droids multiply.

Luke is attended to by robot doctors and surgeons – first at the rebel planet, where he was attacked by a strange animal and almost froze, and again after Vader damaged his arm in the duel. A robot surgeon makes him a cyborg forearm. The doctor droids are humanoid, but the nurse is another kind of vacuum cleaner. Also, on the planet where the trap for Han and his friends were set, is 4-LOM, a protocol droid who turned into a bounty hunter and captured and disassembled C-3PO (later re-assembled by Chewie and R2-D2). At the same time, the linguistic talents of protocol droids are revealed (60 million semantic forms), though their weaknesses remain the same. Forces of the Empire have reconnaissance droids that look like a combination of a large beetle and a vacuum cleaner; they look realistic enough to make the viewer suspect that something similar may actually be used in today's military. R2-D2, the astromech, finally saves everybody by performing an operation for which it has not been programmed. Thus, the variety of droids is widened: There are good droids and evil droids, humanoids and machine-like droids; those limited in their capacities, and those capable of surpassing their programming.

In the third part of the trilogy (*Return of the Jedi*), Luke undertakes the rescue of Han, who has been delivered to the gangster, Jabba, in whose debt he was. At first, the attempt does not go well, and the droids become Jabba's property. They enter a kind of workshop, where both workers and foremen are robots. Disobedient robots are being tortured and punished by supervising robots. But Luke frees Han and returns to Yoda, who has turned 900 and is dying. After his death, the ghost of Kenobi tells Luke to confront his father once again, and also reveals that Leia is Luke's twin sister. The Rebels attack the second Death Star, while Luke engages Vader in another lightsaber duel in the presence of the Emperor, who goads Luke to kill his father, and in this way move to the dark side. When Luke refuses, the Emperor tries to kill him, but Vader switches sides and kills the Emperor. Mortally wounded, but returned to the form of Anakin Skywalker, Luke's father dies in his arms. In the meantime, the droids help the rebels: the protocol droid by becoming a god-like figure within a tribe of teddy-bear-like natives and the astromech by solving all technical problems, at the risk of being destroyed himself. The Rebels demolish the second Death Star and celebrate.

In general, although *SW* does not address the issues of unemployment, it illustrates well the recurring hopes for and fears of robots. Depending on the model and its corresponding purpose, droids could be obedient and expendable, or independent thinkers and therefore potentially dangerous. They all have a vast memory recall, and many are excellent mathematicians. Autonomy or lack of autonomy is both advantageous and disadvantageous: Obedient droids are less efficient; independent-thinking robots can turn treacherous. There is no doubt, however, that C-3PO and R2-D2 are treated like friends by the humans within the trilogy: always rescued when in need and always remembered at critical moments. As to their loyalty, C-3PO has moments of weakness when frightened, whereas R2-D2 is unceasingly loyal. Yet many commentators on the trilogy have wondered why the general sympathy of the public remained with R2-D2 and not with C-3PO. After all, fear and weakness are human traits as well. True, C-3PO also possesses some unattractive human attributes: It is vain, often silly, and quite neurotic.

Beyond this, it should be pointed out that the soldiers of Empire and Darth Vader himself, although human, look like humanoid robots in their armor. This is why *SW* was treated as illustrative of the phenomenon of "uncanny valley." The uncanny valley theory, formulated in the 1970s by Japanese robotics professor Masahiro Mori and introduced to the Anglo-Saxon readership by Polish-British author Jasia Reichardt in 1978, suggested that replicas that look like real human beings are likely to elicit revulsion (MacDorman and Ishiguro, 2006) – and in the case of Darth Vader, fear. Such recent works as *Interstellar* and *Seveneves*, discussed later in this chapter, demonstrate that this lesson was taken seriously by some popular culture and robotics. Yet human replicas are constantly being made, and we return to this issue in the last chapter.

All in all, *SW* is not about work. Perhaps Sunstein was right in claiming that the first trilogy is about fatherhood, redemption, and freedom (2016: 7). Some female viewers may have the impression that there are too many male duels, both individual and in groups. Perhaps *Star Wars* are actually a parable for the origins and development of civilizations in general. After all, as Bruno Latour (1987: 91) observed, "We all believe that negation and thus dialectics are the great masters of history, the midwives of our societies. Nothing is achieved, we all admit too quickly, without struggle, and dispute, and wars, and destruction."

At any rate, the next trilogy (a prequel) is mostly about politics, and the last about the mysteries of universe. Unsurprisingly, works about work are seldom overly popular.

4.6 *BLADE RUNNER* (DO ANDROIDS DREAM OF ELECTRIC SHEEP?, PHILIP K. DICK 1968, RIDLEY SCOTT 1982)

Ridley Scott's 1982 *Blade Runner* was, we thought, an unavoidable choice, because no other film has been mentioned so often in social sciences literature (Joerges and Kress, 2002). Indeed, academics began writing analyses of the film almost as soon as it was released, as it revolves around two crucial themes: the dystopian city of the future[29] and the essence of humanness.[30]

The film is based on a 1968 novel by Phillip Dick, but Ridley introduced many changes and improvisations. (As mentioned, robots are not called androids, but replicants.) The action is set in a dystopian Los Angeles of 2019, and the movie starts with an introductory text:

THE TYRELL CORPORATION advanced Robot evolution into the next NEXUS phase – a being virtually identical to a human – known as a Replicant. The NEXUS 6 *Replicants* were superior in strength and agility, and at least equal in intelligence, to the genetic engineers who created them.
Replicants were used Off-world as slave labor, in the hazardous exploration and colonization of other planets.
After a bloody mutiny by a NEXUS 6 combat team in an Off-world colony, *Replicants* were declared illegal on earth – under penalty of death.
Special police squads – BLADE RUNNER UNITS – had orders to shoot to kill, upon detection, any trespassing *Replicant*.
This was not called execution.
It was called retirement.

NEXUS 6 models were so similar to people that the only way to distinguish them was by using a specially designed Voight-Kampff (V-K) machine test. Replicants differed from real people in two aspects: They had no emotions (or so their creators believed), and they died when they reached four years of age. The humans spoke in a derogatory way of them as "skin-jobs," insinuating an empty inside.

The replicants did the work of serving in the colonies on other planets; but after a rebellion they were not allowed to return to Earth. Yet the

---

[29]   For the review of texts dedicated to this issue and a discussion, see Joerges, 1996, https://www.wzb.eu/www2000/alt/met/pdf/leinwandstaedte.pdf.

[30]   For some early comments on this issue (which was adopted by many other authors), see e.g. Brooks, 1988 and Bullaro, 1993.

NEXUS 6 models wished to prolong their lives and returned to the Earth to "meet their maker" – Dr. Eldon Tyrell. Six of them hijacked a spaceship; two were killed on arrival, but four managed to disperse in LA. An ex-cop, Deckard, who specialized in "retiring" replicants, was bullied back into service. The hunted group acquired a fifth member, an experimental replicant model, Rachael, who did not know that she was not human, as she had implanted memories of Eldon Tyrell's niece and worked as his assistant. By now, she has learned that she is a replicant, however, and has vanished into the city as well.

The replicants kill Tyrell and several of his collaborators and are on the verge of killing Deckard, but Rachael saves him. In turn, he saves Rachael, and they both vanish at the end of the film. (The endings have been changed in the seven different cuts of the film.)[31]

Replicants working in colonies had various specialties, and the four escapees are no exception:

- Roy (the leader of the fugitives) was a self-sufficient combat model for the colonization defense program (Physical-A, Mental-A, serial number N6MAA10816).
- Pris was a "basic pleasure model" for military personnel (Physical-A, Mental-B, N6FAB21416). After the escape, she worked as a "woman-with-a-snake" in a night club.
- Zhora was trained for a murder squad (Physical-A, Mental-B, N6FAB61216).
- Leon was a combat model and a loader of nuclear fission materials (Physical-A, Mental-C, N6MAC41717).

As to humanness, the (V-K) machine test would quickly reveal a Mental-C replicant, like Leon, but it was not as easy with Rachael. In fact, although the V-K machine was obviously a variation on the Turing test, one wonders if Ridley Scott wasn't – intentionally or not – poking fun at the expense of intelligence tests, known for their cultural inadequacy. Rachael fails to answer the question of what she would do were she invited for a dinner where a dog was served as the main dish ...

---

[31] After the 1981 film, there was an ongoing debate about whether Deckard was a human or a replicant. Allegedly, Ridley Scott claimed that in his opinion, Deckard was a replicant, whereas Harrison Ford, who plays Deckard, insisted that he was a human; the 2017 sequel made his humanness obvious.

The final test is obvious, and most poetically formulated by the dying Roy:

> I've seen things you people wouldn't believe. Attack ships on fire off the shoulder of Orion; I watched C-beams glitter in the dark near the Tannhauser Gate. All those moments will be lost in time like tears in rain. [He cries, rain washing off his tears]

So yes, replicants have feelings, and apparently deeper and more human feelings than the humans who did not hesitate to exploit them – just as they exploited slaves. (The analogy is raised several times in the film.) The replicants show compassion and concern for one another, obvious characteristics when they are juxtaposed against human characters, who lack sympathy, like the cold and impersonal mass of humanity on the streets. As to love, it is difficult to say, as Rachael may have saved Deckard in order to make him her debtor, and her love declarations, obviously forced by him, sound rather robotic. In the epoch of #metoo, his professional future would be in question. (See also Williams, 2017, on the feminist critique of films *noir*.)

All in all, it is difficult not to agree with Douglas E. Williams (2017), who has summarized the impact of the 1982 *Blade Runner*:

> Despite the seeming simplicity of its plot, the stylistic complexity, ideological ambiguity and frequently searching, philosophical nature of the sparse dialogue we are presented with, make Blade Runner a film that has much to teach, or at least worry, us about unprecedented and life-threatening complexities of our technologies, the social and political definition of their deployment and development, and the incoherence of our currently stereotypical attempts to escape from the repercussions of the world we see taking shape before our eyes.[32]

As in so many other sci-fi films, the robots of *Blade Runner* have performed revolting, dirty, dull, and physically dangerous tasks that humans could or would not perform. But this is not seen in the film as either good or bad in itself. Yet the film arouses compassion for replicants, whose life span was programmed by their corporate inventor.

From our point of view, the 1982 *Blade Runner* reformulates the query posed in *R.U.R.* and arises again and again: "What if robots and humans

---

[32]   http://scrapsfromtheloft.com/2017/07/06/ideology-dystopia-interpretation - blade-runner/, accessed November 7, 2017.

blur, and what if and when robots emerge as superior entities?" The film suggests that the replicants are morally superior, but offers no conclusion as to human–robot relationships that should follow. It ends in a manner appropriate for an escapist fairy tale.

4.7   *SNOW CRASH* (NEAL STEPHENSON, 1992)

Popular cultural works concerning robotization were not prominent in the decade separating *Blade Runner* from *Snow Crash*, perhaps because the 1980s were seen as a "winter period" in AI development (Crevier, 1993).

Snow Crash is mostly about hackers, virtual reality, avatars, and the breakdown of cyberspace; robots in the meaning of the word we are using here seem largely absent. Yet they are present, and at least two types are noteworthy. The first type is notable precisely because these robots are so different from both humanoids and "the vacuum-cleaners." Still, Stephenson referred to them as robots:

> In a Mr. Lee's Greater Hong Kong franchise in Phoenix, Arizona, Ng Security Industries Semi-Autonomous Guard Unit B-782 comes awake.
>
>   The factory that put him together thinks of him as a robot named Number B-782. But he thinks of himself as a pit bullterrier named Fido (p. 249)

There is no doubt about the fact that Fido is working:

> He has an important job: Protect the yard. Sometimes people come in and out of the yard. Most of the time, they are good people, and he does not bother them. He doesn't know why they are good people. He just knows it. Sometimes they are bad people, and he has to do bad things to them to make them go away. This is fitting and proper.
>
>   Out in the world beyond his yard, there are other yards with other doggies just like him. They aren't nasty dogs. They are all his friends. (…) He belongs to a big pack of nice doggies. (p. 89)

"Nice doggies," known generally as Rat Things, are guards. Perhaps they could be called cyborgs rather than robots, although that raises a question: If their mechanical parts dominate their organic parts, are these creatures cyborgs or robots? Perhaps it should be added that Ng, the owner of Ng Security, is himself such a creature, after the damages to his body during the Vietnam War.

When Y.T., the Kourier (the courier), one of the main characters in *Snow Crash*, learns that Rat Things are made from dog parts, she thinks it is cruel. Ng explains to her why she is wrong:

> "Your mistake," Ng says, "is that you think that all mechanically assisted organisms – like me – are pathetic cripples. In fact, we are better than we were before."
> "Where do you get the pit bulls from?"
> "An incredible number of them are abandoned every day, in cities all over the place."
> "You cut up pound puppies?"
> "We save abandoned dogs from certain extinction and send them to what amounts to dog heaven." (p. 248)

It appears that the preservation of dog parts serves at least two functions. One, it permits Rat Dogs to enjoy life: when not on active duty, they live in what truly amounts to a dog heaven.

> Ng Security Industries Semi-Autonomous Guard Unit #A-367 lives in a pleasant black-and-white Metaverse [virtual reality] where porterhouse steaks grow on trees, dangling at head level from low branches, and blood-drenched Frisbees fly through the crisp, cool air for no reason at all, until you catch them. (p. 89)

When at work, they are still enjoying themselves ("Can't you imagine how liberating it is for a pit bull-terrier to be capable of running seven hundred miles an hour?" p. 248). Furthermore, a Rat Thing preserves one important characteristic of real dogs: loyalty to (good) people. In fact, Y.T. and her boyfriend once saved Fido; the dog remembers it and is always ready to protect her. And it is Fido who delivers justice in the final scene.

There are other robots in *Snow Crash*, usually security guards, most of them in virtual reality as avatars.

> "Daemon" is an old piece of jargon from the UNIX operating system, where it referred to a piece of low-level utility software, a fundamental part of the operating system. In The Black Sun [a pub in virtual reality], a demon is like an avatar, but it does not represent a human being. (...) The Black Sun has a number of daemons that serve imaginary drinks to the patrons and run little errands for people. (p. 55)

Most daemons look like people, though, and not all of them are low-level software. The one that is truly remarkable is the Librarian – a kind of a robot every scientist would be only too happy to possess.

> The Librarian daemon looks like a pleasant, silver-haired, bearded man with bright blue eyes, wearing a V-neck sweater over a work shirt, with a coarsely woven, tweedy-looking wool tie. (…) Even though he's just a piece of software, he has reasons to be cheerful; he can move through the nearly infinite stacks of information in the Library with the agility of a spider dancing across a vast web of cross-references. (…) the only thing he can't do is think. (p. 107)

A browser in humanoid shape then. And although, according to Stephenson, the Librarian cannot think, the robot does not offer a mere page of links ordered according to who paid more money to Google: It offers correct answers to any question the user may ask. What is more, it is able to develop its skills:

> "You're a pretty decent piece of ware. Who wrote you, anyway?"
> "For the most part I write myself," the Librarian says. "That is, I have an innate ability to learn from experience. But this ability was originally coded into me by my creator." (p. 109)

Stephenson was here some thirty years ahead of the actual AI developments, but of course this trait has been discussed, planned for, or at least hoped for from the outset.

The Librarian's only fault is that it imitates real librarians only too well: It moves so quietly that the user does not hear it and wishes for more noise to avoid being startled. Neither does the robot have a memory; the Library is its memory, and it can recall only what is there. Still, the users may not be sure about what the Librarian can or cannot do.

> He suspects that the Librarian may be pulling his leg, playing him for a fool. But he knows that the Librarian, however convincingly rendered he may be, is just a piece of software and cannot actually do such things. (p. 209)

Can't he/it do that, though? This is a new kind of fear, not predicted by Asimov in his laws of robotics: that robots, or quasi-robots, can ridicule humans.

It should be added that compared to *Seveneves* (2015), in which robots (of a peculiar kind) play a truly important role, the robots in *Snow Crash* are mostly narrative devices. The Librarian fulfills a critical function in that (like in all Stephenson's books) the robot can deliver a significant summary of research results (in this case, on Sumerian tradition, Babel Tower, and language history in general). Rat Things can be seen as a variation of one of the most popular job for robots – that of security guards. Yet both the suspect tendency of the Librarian to mock its user and the dogs' tendency to reward good conduct with loyalty are interesting, albeit small, additions to the robotization debate.

4.8 *THE MATRIX* (LARRY AND ANDY WACHOWSKI, 1998)

The Matrix is about the most extreme fear that humans have toward their robotic creations: In this movie, Artificial Intelligence attacked the humans and started growing human bodies for the source of energy they needed. (At a certain point, Morpheus, one of the characters who rebels against the robots, shows a battery to Neo, the main character and the future savior, to explain to him the role that human bodies play in 2199.) In order to prevent humans from resisting and rebelling, the AIs created a simulation of a real world, which keeps humans happy, and which is under total control of the AI. If this sounds like the most unrealistic fantasy, it is enough to remind readers that Elon Musk recently claimed that "There's a billion to one chance we're living in base reality"(which, he thinks, is better than being dead[33]).

In the movie, robots do all the things that humans cannot (until they acquire superhuman power, like Neo does). In *The Matrix*, all security services are humanoid robots, as are the police, although they are better masquerading as humans (all agents look almost the same). They are not so much replicants as "sentient programs," to quote Morpheus again. There are a great many other robots whose shape and form depends on their function. A bugging robot looks like a scorpion. (It gets inside a bugged person via the navel.) Robots meant to destroy the rebel hovercraft are called sentinels or "squiddies," because they look like squids, and their function is to "search and destroy," These are autonomous killing machines that patrol the ancient sewers of the dead human cities in search of Zion's hovercrafts. (Zion is the last colony of real humans,

---

[33] http://www.theverge.com/2016/6/2/11837874/elon-musk-says-odds -living-in-simulation, accessed March 1, 2017.

living deep inside the Earth, where it is still warm.[34]) Or the squiddies may be searching for wandering, defenseless human beings who, for some reason or another, are walking in the tunnels. Squiddies' tentacles are needed as audio sensors, able to pick up all sounds, so that Zion's ships must shut down power when the squiddies approach. Close up, their tentacles change into sharp claws, drilling through the ship's hull or killing the humans. Even rebels have robots for some more basic functions, like transporting and collecting.

The commentators, human or not, are often quite sarcastic about the humans. Here is Morpheus again:

> We don't know who struck first, us or them. But we know that it was us that scorched the sky. At the time they were dependent on solar power and it was believed that they would be unable to survive without an energy source as abundant as the sun. Throughout human history, we have been dependent on machines to survive. Fate it seems is not without a sense of irony.

Now the machines use humans in order to survive. What is worse, robots' opinions of humans as workers is not high: "Never send a human to do a machine's job," says Agent Smith.

But robots are not only the bad guys. In fact, Agent Smith, in telling the history of the Matrix, says that it was originally supposed to be a perfect world, full of happiness. Alas, it did not work. Apparently, humans cannot live without suffering and misery, so the AIs simply provided them with what they wanted.

In later sequels, it turns out that even the benevolent Oracle was a machine, but one that specialized in human psychology and understood its complicated and sometimes contradictory nature. Thus, she was able to give them philosophical advice, which they fulfilled by opposing it.

In the original of *The Matrix*, there are not many more insights, as the major part of the movie is dedicated to various fights and duels, which seem to suggest that fighting is what robots and humans alike are most fond of. (These are mostly duels between male characters, though Trinity contributes as well.) Furthermore, as Morpheus is a god of dreams, it may mean that his idea of a savior coming was but a dream.

---

[34] For a long time, and at least since the times of Gabriel Tarde (see his sci-fi story, *Underground man*, 1896/1905), it was believed that the environmental catastrophe would consist of global cooling rather than global warming.

4.9   THE STEPFORD WIVES (IRA LEVIN, 1972; FRANK OZ, 2004)

In 1988, in the year that allegedly was the beginning of another "winter" in the development of AI, independent German film director Peter Krieg made a film essay called *Machine Dreams*. Krieg's films were cinematic dissertations; he had also made one on money and one on chaos theory. *Machine Dreams* included a thesis on the genesis and development of technology, a rich field material, and quotes from scientific literature delivered by the scholars themselves. It ended with a theory about the development of machines as a realization of both dreams and nightmares of men.[35] It unfolded as follows: Men constructed machines to escape their biological nature (of which women play a large part). This technical "second nature" brought them more disappointment than relief, however, because, according to Krieg, projected dreams and nightmares are apt to return. Indeed, our analysis tends to confirm his observation.

Within this general thesis or plot were several subplots, situated historically. One of the main drives behind the construction of machines was to relieve humans of heavy menial work; once successful, they moved to the mechanizing of lighter menial work, like household work.[36] Another drive was to protect men from threat; and as men feel threatened by women, replacing women as sex objects with sex machines was the next step. If one develops this logic to its absurd consequence, housewives can be seen as a combination of household machines and sex objects. Thus, Stepford wives.

The topic of the original novel, Ira Levin's book from 1972 was, in our reading, the rising feminism, or women's liberation, as it was then called. After all, the book begins with a quote from Simone de Beauvoir's *The Second Sex* (1949).

There are two main points to the book, and Ira Levin proved to be right about both of them. One is that men will not lightly accept women's liberation – especially their liberation from household duties, including sexual services. They will fight back. The other point is that this libera-

---

[35]   Literally men: "All machines are female, because men dream of them," Krieg says in the film.

[36]   Krieg was obviously ignorant of Ruth Schwartz Cowan's work (1985), *More work for mother: The ironies of household technology from the open hearth to the microwave.*

tion is inevitable. They would have to kill women – and/or turn them into robots – to stop it.

Yet technology does not play an important role in the book; it is merely a prop necessary for the plot. The plot involves a professional photographer, Joanne Eberhart, who has just moved home to Stepford with her family. All the women she meets are somewhat peculiar, and she finds it difficult to make new friends. Women in Stepford do not chat and drink coffee together: They have a great deal of cleaning and housework to do. Joanne and her only friend, another professional woman named Bobbie, try to decipher the situation and discover that the Stepford housewives used to belong to a powerful Women's Association, and that after Betty Friedan gave a talk there, a Men's Association was formed, and women's behavior started to change drastically.

Levin's book actually reverts to the plot of *R.U.R.*; after all, Čapek's robots were organic products. Levin's innovation consisted of relocating the conflict: It was no longer between robots and people or between industrialists and workers, but between men and women. In Čapek's play, the robots win; in Levin's book, the women lose, but both endings are absurd, as they were intended to be. The purpose was to force the spectators or the readers to reflect over issues that could prove disturbing.

The novel is short, which probably prompted the subsequent film-makers to extend it, at the same time giving them enough space to do it the way they preferred. The movie from 1975 (screenwriter William Goldman, director Bryan Forbes) focused on portraying the USA as obsessed by commercials. The other two themes – technology and women – are marginal. Technology is threatening: Anything of importance is made manually, and men dealing with technology are sinister. Computer and various lab companies have sinister, black-and-white signboards, unlike everything else in the movie, which is colorful. The women in the film are real, and by the end of the movie, it is difficult to combat the feeling that they get what they deserve. They seem to be intellectually handicapped, or at least made so by their love of their spouses and children.

The next remake of *Stepford Wives* (2004) occurred at a time when Levin's claims seemed prophetic. Women's liberation had advanced, and technology had taken over the society, used by both men and women. The points that Levin had made could not be made again, so the plot was rearranged accordingly.

After being fired as president of a television network, Joanna has a nervous breakdown, and her husband Walter takes her to a simple

Connecticut town called Stepford to recuperate. But Stepford is a little strange: The husbands gather at a men's club, whereas the wives – all in bright summer frocks and constantly smiling – only exercise and cook pastries. Joanna, along with other new arrivals, Bobbie and Roger, soon discovers that the mastermind of Stepford has used cybernetics to "improve" womankind.

The motivation of the Stepford men returns to the one hinted at by Levin, but is more convincing. In the 1975 version they were a bunch of weird technos with mean ideas; in 2004 they are less successful husbands of successful wives. The technology portrayed in the movie is complex and plays a significant role in the plot, and at the genius end of it is a woman. In addition, the idea of a house-machine is made equal, because a gay partner is also remade into such a model.

All in all, the 2004 version comes closest to Peter Krieg's thesis. Technology is used to rid human life of imperfection ("biological nature"), but the key to happiness lies in accepting imperfections, not in getting rid of them. Yet the topic of "women-as-technology" is especially interesting, although it attracted little attention from the reviewers. This is an ancient topic, after all: If Eve was made of Adam's rib, women are like Dolly the sheep, cloned from a bit of man, to serve him in life. It is a matter of accessible technology whether they are made of metal and springs, like a long series of antique docks shown in Peter Krieg's film; of plastic and computers, like Japanese robots in the same film; or are brain-engineered cyborgs, as in the *Stepford Wives* of 2004. Here, the symbolic border that Philip K. Dick emphasized is crossed again, but in a direction opposite to that in most sci-fi works: It is people who become robot-like, not robots that become human-like. (This was what Braverman, 1974, feared, too.)

One dominant impression is that the novelist and the filmmakers did not know much about the household as a workplace, as they reproduced various stereotypes about the organization of a household. The 2004 movie opens with a 1950s-style commercial, in which new household machines play the main role. In this way, the movie establishes an historical background, alluding to the rationalization of housework in a Tayloristic spirit. In Stepford, however, there is no need for the new machines, because women *are* machines. At the same time, the traditional role of a housewife who can do anything is preserved.

The mechanization of the household held the same double message at the time of its introduction. As Ruth Cowan Schwartz (1985) demonstrated, household technology, intended to relieve women of heavy duties, relieved men of heavyweight duties, and children of light household duties. Women, on the other hand, became even busier, as the standards of a clean, effective household skyrocketed. No wonder the Stepford wives didn't have time to chat! As Boel Berner (1996) reminded her readers, housewives in the rationalized society were supposed to acquire new technical competence, setting them on par with their technically minded husbands. But were the machines intended to keep women at home, or were they supposed to free women to assume jobs in the public sphere?

In the 2004 version, the "real" women left the housework to men so they could pursue their careers without concerning themselves about family and home. Joanna takes for granted her hi-tech "smart home" and her husband's ability to use the controls. Yet women of the 1950s and the 1960s also played a significant role in the household – not as the masters, but as the organizers (Berner, 1996: 122), and in this function they were irreplaceable. When Joanna lost her job, she had no power platform whatsoever and was unable to answer her husband's accusation that she could be defective. Joanna's lack of familiarity with the household technology turned it into her foe. The talking fridge reminded her of her shortcomings and the security system refused to let her in.

Stepford husbands were clearly not afraid that their robotic wives would turn against them, like robots in *Terminator*, *Blade Runner*, and *RoboCop* had done. The traditional assumption that people control the robots and not the other way around has not been challenged. Yet an interesting twist in the 2004 version is that it is a woman (played by Glenn Close) who is finally responsible for the robotization of the women. She thinks that everything was better before women left their traditional household roles. She used to be a talented researcher in the field of brain surgery and cybertechnology, and she applies her expertise to turn back the clock.

Intentionally or unintentionally, this is yet another way in which the movie shows that women's familiarity with technology is a serious threat to the patriarchs. *Stepford Wives*, throughout its variations, addressed several topics that do not cease to be relevant: The differences between public and private workplaces, the promises and traps of professional competition between men and women, and the hopes and fears about technologies.

A contemporary public may see the "household machine hopes" as a thing of the past, a historical curiosity. Not so with another part of machine dreams: cyborgs and androids as wives, lovers, and work colleagues. *Stepford Wives* in one form or another has existed for nearly a half century. To what extent does the development of its characters reflect the developments in the society at large?

Feminists have since started talking of a backlash, and, indeed, it is quite possible that in the twenty-first century women can be imprisoned at home, their political and educational rights taken away. Changes do occur, but not always go forward ...

In 1983, Cynthia Cockburn and her collaborators interviewed an advertising worker who said "It would be quite unthinkable to present a publicity (...) where the woman, if she was visible in the picture, was not the one who did the kitchen work" (Cockburn, 1996: 24). If this advertising man had not retired, he would not be saying the same thing now. We are all used to publicity showing women in front of computers (with eyeglasses signaling intellectual aptitude) and men in aprons in front of (induction) kitchens. Yet "Stepford wives" has become a label in the USA; Stepford is a marker for small, conservative suburbs that emerge around big cities.

But there are more and rather unpleasant analogies between the world of today and the original Stepford wives, and not only in the USA. According to Rappe and Strannegård (2004), more and more people in Sweden want to have a clean house or an even "cleaner house," and fewer and fewer will be doing that cleaning themselves. Robotic vacuum cleaners still do not do a very good of cleaning the corners. As Ehrenreich and Hochschild noted in 2002, one solution is immigrant women, who clean and iron, take care of children and the elderly, and provide sexual services. Like robots, they are not on the same emotional and intellectual level as their masters/employers (one can't talk with them), and they raise the same anxieties. What happens if they hurt themselves/break? Will it be possible to get a new model quickly? What if they stage a revolution? If one could only impose Asimov's laws on them!

The situation is presently becoming more acute, and it does not concern only women. Who is more dangerous: immigrants or robots? Who is more prone to rebellion? Can robots fill the gap in the workforce if immigrants won't? This topic will return in both the media and social science works.

4.10 *BIG HERO 6* (MARVEL COMICS 1998, DISNEY 2014)

There are at least three reasons for including an animated movie here. First, it was highly popular, to put it mildly: It was the highest-grossing animated film of 2014, with sales of over $500 million worldwide.[37] Second, it was especially popular among young people – the people who will decide the fate of the robots of the future. Third, the main robot in the film is (basically) a medical robot – the job that seems to be the main novelty in the use of robots, as compared to industrial robots of yesteryear.

The movie begins with a botfight – the equivalent of dogfight – obviously, an interest for the ne'er-do-wells. Unfortunately, and much to the chagrin of his older brother, Tadashi, an extremely talented young Hiro frequents botfights, and his clever bots are continually winning against those of various villains. Using subterfuge, Tadashi succeeds in taking Hiro to a "nerd lab," in which a group of young people works under the guidance of Professor Callaghan; "we push the boundaries of robotics here," says Tadashi proudly.

Tadashi's own project is Baymax, an inflatable medical robot, looking like an enormous human-shaped balloon, with inside equipment that includes all possible diagnoses and 10,000 medical procedures for both physical and psychological conditions. Hiro is so impressed that he decides to apply to the School that educates the "nerds." In order to prepare his entrance work, he goes to a kind of garage (as readers will know, all important digital inventions were made in garages) and constructs a microbot. A microbot is a larger version of a nanorobot in that it is visible with naked eye; but like nanorobots, it can take any shape desired by its operator. (Stephenson's novel, discussed at the end of this chapter, also makes use of nanorobots. In fact, the movie contains several allusions to Stephenson's works). Hiro wins the competition and is accepted by the School, and the CEO of Krei Company wants to buy his invention. Professor Callaghan encourages him to decline the offer and enter the School; the CEO attempts to steal the microbot, but apparently fails.

The same night a fire starts in the School; Tadashi tries to save the Professor, but both die in the fire. Hiro is so despondent that he wants

---

[37] https://en.wikipedia.org/wiki/Big_Hero_6_(film), accessed July 15, 2017.

to drop the School and return to botfights, but he hurts his foot on the way there. His cry is heard by Baymax, which turns out to be in Hiro and Tadashi's home. The robot diagnoses Hiro's physical and psychological pain and gives him a lecture on the dangers of puberty. (Baymax utters many psychological platitudes throughout the movie, but it is difficult to know if the intention is satirical.)

Baymax also discovers that the microbot is moving as if intending to go places, so the big robot follows the little robot through the streets of San Fransokyo (a futuristic combination of San Francisco and Tokyo), Hiro behind them. They end up in an old factory building and discover that somebody has undertaken large-scale production of microbots. They are attacked by microbots that are guided by a man in a Kabuki mask. They go to the police but are not believed.

Baymax realizes that his batteries are down; consequently, he behaves like a drunk, and Hiro has to smuggle him to his room so his aunt will not see them. (Unlike her nephews and their chums, she simply works in cafeteria and cooks dinners at home.) Once charged, Baymax looks for prescriptions on how to manage a loss, and discovers that compassion, companionship, and physical reassurance are needed. While hugging Hiro, Baymax asks for help from Tadashi's colleagues from the Nerd Lab (thus the six in the title – two men and two women join in).

Hiro discovers that the fire was not an accident and suspects Krei. He updates Baymax to become a warrior, teaches him karate, and gives him an order to go and get "that guy in the Kabuki mask." The two follow the Kabuki man and almost fall off the edge of a cliff into the water when he vanishes. (Baymax: "Always wait one hour after eating before swimming.") When Kabuki and his microbots turn back to attack them, Hiro and Baymax discover that the lab group has been following them in a little car. A chase ensues, which gets serious only when one of the women takes over the wheel. The Kabuki man manages to push the car with all of them in it into the ocean, but the balloon-like Baymax saves them.

They hide in the house of one of the guys – a posh villa with a butler. Hiro updates them all on various kinds of cyborg warriors, and they test their capacities on the butler. This time, Baymax becomes a super-Superman, and Hiro puts the black-and-red killer SIM card next to its green "medical" card. Hiro can fly to the top of the Golden Bridge, and all over San Fransokyo on Baymax's back. Baymax is also able to discover the place where the Kabuki man is hiding by scanning all the bodies in the city. The team arrives at an island where Krei's factory is located and discovers a video showing that Krei was working with teleportation and has sent a young woman named Abigail into space. The experiment did not work and the woman was lost.

The Kabuki man shows up, and a prolonged fight ensues. Hiro gives Baymax the order to destroy, but the women know better, remove the killer card, and block the possibility of changing the programming. The Kabuki man escapes.

To comfort Hiro, Baymax shows him a video of Tadashi's work with his invention, which convinces Hiro that the robot's task is to heal and help, not to destroy. The only thing that is needed is to take the mask off the Kabuki man, so that he will not be able to command his microbots. The team eventually manages to do that, upon which they discover that Professor Callaghan is the man behind the Kabuki mask, that Abigail was his daughter, and that he is seeking revenge. It was he who stole Hiro's microbot and allowed Tadashi to die. The Professor gets the mask back, and the fight continues, because the team is able to find new angles. (Again, a joke on management platitudes or a serious advice?)

Baymax is able to scan outer space, where he discovers a human being. Abigail is alive. Hiro and the robot get into outer space and find Abigail, but Baymax suffers from a crash and breaks into parts. It asks Hiro to close him down, which can be achieved by saying "I am satisfied with your care." Although Hiro's heart is broken, he says the words. He brings Abigail back to the world, and the police take Professor Callaghan into custody. Only when drinking coffee in his aunt's cafeteria, does Hiro discover that the remaining part of Baymax, a fist, holds its programming card. The robot can be reproduced.

The US critics were positive. A typical review said that the movie "offers something for everyone: action, camaraderie, superheroes and villains. But mostly, Baymax offers a compassionate and healing voice for those suffering, and a hug that can be felt through the screen."[38]

As it often happens, some European critics begged to differ. Here is a Norwegian opinion:

> Big Hero 6 is best in the two first acts when the young boy and the robot draw lines and become better acquainted with each other. I was disappointed that the film did not focus a little more on the grieving process after the young boy

---

[38] http://www.dfw.com/2014/11/06/941360/movie-review-big-hero-6.html, accessed March 15, 2017.

had lost his brother; it did not take many minutes before it was forgotten and laughter and fun took over. (…)
The end is cowardly, very cowardly. I realize why one chooses a hopeless end like this in children's films, but as an adult I am always disappointed.[39]

The Italian review is even harsher:

That Disney Animation Studios did some sort of Avengers for a younger audience is one thing that is perplexing, but that they do so in a manner so bland and uninteresting is really depressing. Yet to begin with, the construction of the universe in which the film is set – a future world in which Japanese culture strongly influences the United States – makes obvious the main problem of the project: an attempt to build the story around the marketing potential instead of the dramaturgical necessities.[40]

Differences between the US and the European reviews were only to be expected – although quite a few Swedish reviewers were enchanted, and some US reviewers agreed with the Europeans. ("The character is a windfall of laughs, emotion, and merchandising potential – in short, a marketer's dream."[41])
In our opinion, Baymax was cleverly designed as a medical robot. Its balloon-like body meant that it could embrace humans, getting close to their bodies without hurting them. Its declared capacities were incredible. Yet in the movie its talents were used primarily in chases and fights, even if the fights were more sophisticated than botfights, as they included various clever moves, and their goal was "to help human beings." (Before each step, Baymax asks Hiro if he will feel better afterwards.) But fights comprised the largest part of the movie. One observation is undoubtedly correct: Japan will have much to say about the direction in which the construction of robots will take.

---

[39]   http://dvd-world.biz/filmblogg/?p=23263, accessed March 15, 2017.
[40]   http://www.cinefile.biz/big-hero-6-di-don-hall-chris-williams,   accessed March 15, 2017.
[41]   http://www.cinemixtape.com/movie-reviews/big-hero-6/, accessed March 15, 2017.

4.11 *INTERSTELLAR* (CHRISTOPHER NOLAN, 2014)

The role robots play in *Interstellar* is quite limited. Still, it is worthy of attention for at least two reasons: their physical build and their humor. There is nothing humanoid in their shape. They are rectangular blocks of metal, comprising four panels that can move independently. The two extremes operate like arms and legs, but when needed, the whole thing converts into a kind of windmill, with all the four panels revolving. The center panels function as a screen on which information is visible. Inside are many cables and connections, visible when robots are being repaired or destroyed. Furthermore, their funny and cheeky retorts to their human masters, completely unlike the mechanical voices that the viewers are used to hearing, add humor to the story.

The movie starts with a post-apocalyptic landscape in US. The only thing that can be cultivated is corn, humans suffer from horrible dust storms, and it is known that soon even the corn will die out. The main character, Joseph Cooper, lives with his two children and his father-in-law. His wife died earlier, and his son is supposed to continue his work as a farmer. Cooper had been a pilot, but his career ended in an accident that is not explained. His younger daughter, Murphy, complains of hearing and seeing a ghost in her bedroom. It moves books, and she tries to figure out what could be its message – without much success, until another dust storm leaves a peculiar sand pattern on the floor. Cooper and Murphy manage to decipher it; these are coordinates of a place that Cooper is determined to investigate. Murphy is forbidden to follow him, but she does by hiding in the pickup.

The place turns out to be a facility of NASA, which still operates in hiding. Everybody there knows about Cooper's piloting skills. Cooper meets Professor Brand, whom he has known previously, and who continues to work on spaceships in hiding. Brand convinces Cooper that he needs to perform yet another piloting operation, "not to save the world, but to leave it." NASA has discovered a shortcut to another galaxy that contains several planets similar to Earth. Ships were sent there to investigate, and some of the scouts sent back positive messages. Cooper and his crew are to check those planets, to see which of them could be the destination of people from the doomed Earth.

Cooper also meets a robot called TARS, which is one of former U.S. Marine Corps tactical robots that now works for NASA. Cooper's immediate association is with a vacuum cleaner (an obvious allusion to *Star Wars*). When he discovers that the robot has a sense of humor, edging on sarcasm, Cooper asks TARS how that is possible, to which the robot explains that it has been programmed with 100 percent human humor, but only 9 percent honesty, because diplomacy is often better than straightforward answers.

Even though Murphy does not want Cooper to join the mission (she claims that the ghost left a message saying "STAY"!), he decides to go. He leaves on the spaceship Endurance, in the company of Professor Brand's daughter, Amelia Brand, along with two other human collaborators, Doyle and Romilly. On board, Cooper meets CASE, another robot that is less talkative than TARS but an excellent co-pilot. They travel through the wormhole and arrive at the other galaxy, where they are to visit three planets. One of the persons sent there seems to be a good friend of Amelia, and Cooper asks TARS if they are an item. TARS answers that his discretion programming is also 100 percent – no gossip allowed.

TARS and CASE, which look the same, have unhuman shapes, but strongly human attributes, including different personalities. TARS does not seem to like Cooper, whereas CASE collaborates without comment.

They decide to go first to the planet Miller, so-called from the surname of a woman who went there – a planet where an hour is equivalent of seven years on the Earth. It turns out that enormous waves killed Miller and destroyed her equipment. The waves are about to attack the vehicle on which Amelia and Doyle arrived for reconnaissance. Cooper gives CASE the order to "Go and get her," and the robot, turning into a windmill, manages to save her, whereas Doyle is taken away by the wave.

They go back to the Endurance, on which Romilly has aged 23 years. They do not have enough fuel to visit both planets and return home, so they need to choose which of the two planets to target. Amelia, guided by loving intuition, wants to go to the planet where her beloved Edmund is, but Cooper decides, rationally, to select the planet from which Dr. Mann sent very attractive reports. Still, Amelia believes that only love can cross time and space.[42]

Still on the Endurance, they decide that TARS should be sent as a probe into the black hole (called Gargantua) because the secret of

---

[42] *Interstellar* contains bits of typical US sentimentality concerning the power of feelings towards lovers and children, but they are easy to hop over, and they are not particularly disturbing.

gravity is apparently hidden there. Amelia protests, as TARS may not come back from the excursion, to which TARS responds, "Don't forget that I am a robot, and we do as we are told."

In the meantime, TARS charts the course to Dr. Mann's planet. (When Cooper gives it an order, it responds "Roger that, Cooper.") Arriving there, they discover another robot of the same type called KIPP, which was decommissioned. After having de-hibernated Dr. Mann, they discover that he is a cheater who faked his report in order to be saved, and the planet is completely uninhabitable. Dr. Mann tries to kill Cooper, but Cooper manages to defend himself and asks Amelia for help. She arrives with CASE, they hear an explosion from Dr. Mann's base, and TARS appears and apologizes for being unable to save Romilly, who died there.

Dr. Mann is trying to dock into the Endurance, but Cooper engages TARS for help. He asks the robot: "What is your trust setting, TARS?" "Higher than yours, apparently." answers TARS. While Dr. Mann fails the docking, but puts the Endurance into a spin, Cooper tells CASE to dock their vehicle. "It is not possible," says CASE, to which Cooper answers, "No, but it is necessary." They arrive safely at the Endurance. The new plan is to approach the Gargantua as close they safely can, to travel on the strength of the black hole, and then to separate and go to Edmund's planet, saving the fuel for the return home. TARS needs to be sacrificed at the last moment, however, to which it says, "That's what robots are for." It also says, "Good-bye Dr. Brand" to Amelia, and somewhat strangely: "See you on the other side, Cooper." And so it turns out that Cooper has to join him into the black hole.

Once he has stopped moving in Gargantua, Cooper calls TARS, but gets no answer. Instead, he discovers himself to be on the other side of his daughter Murphy's bookshelf. He has travelled back in time. He leaves the message "STAY," but TARS finds him and informs him that "they" are saving them, and that the message to Earth should be sent with gravity. TARS tries to explain to Cooper that "they" didn't bring them to this place to change the past, and Cooper starts to understand that "they" are "us" – people from the successful future. Cooper and TARS decide that the secret of gravity that they discovered in the black hole can be conveyed to the adult Murphy, now a first-class space scientist, with Morse code on the second hand of the watch Cooper left for his daughter to remember him.

The movie ends with the 124-year-old Cooper landing on what is called "Cooper Station," in honor of his daughter, who did solve the gravity problem and helped to move people from the Earth. She was in a cryonic sleep for two years, waiting for him to come to say goodbye before she died. Cooper then returns to Amelia (who discovered that Edmund was dead, but the planet was habitable) to help her continue their task. He restarts TARS, which now has 95 percent honesty but only 75 percent humor and 60 percent autodestruct. Cooper gives him the nickname "Slick." (It needs to be added that all the robots speak with male voices: There seems to be a pervasive tendency to male gendering of robots in the film.)

It is hard not to agree with Eric Sofge (2014), when he reminded the readers of *Popular Science* that humans will travel into space together with robots. After all, robots have already been to Mars. But it is still unclear what shape will they have and what functions they will be able to perform.

> Would they be humanoids, like NASA's present-day experimental bot, Robonaut 2, which is currently being tested aboard the International Space Station? Or would they be more alien themselves, with bodies and behaviors that support humans, without physically mimicking them? In (…) *Interstellar*, we see the latter option. The robots that accompany a manned expedition to another world are monolithic space oddities, rectangular slabs whose plank-like segments can decouple and rotate to pull off a variety of actions.[43]

In Sofge's opinion, *Interstellar* robots are "gorgeous and silly." Perhaps, although it is difficult to understand how they can perform tasks requiring hands and fingers. Yet director Nolan's choice only revokes the old issue of the creepiness of humanoid robots versus the alienness of non-humanoid robots.

The next popular science fiction work seems to solve this problem convincingly in the context of space travel, but perhaps the solution is not advisable in healthcare and social care.

4.12   *SEVENEVES* (NEAL STEPHENSON, 2015)

Neal Stephenson stands out, like Arthur C. Clarke in his time, for including many actual scientific research results in his science fiction.[44] In *Seveneves* there is so much science – space science – that it seems

---

[43]   http://www.popsci.com/article/technology/co-robots-interstellar-are-gorgeous-and-silly, accessed March 31, 2017.

[44]   See also his joint initiative with Arizona State University, https://en.wikipedia.org/wiki/Project_Hieroglyph, accessed January 6, 2018.

that the author sometimes forgot that he was writing a work of fiction.[45] Yet we decided to include it in our analysis, although it is an exception – the only work in this chapter that is unlikely (at almost 900 pages) to become a bestseller. There is a film in the making, though, directed by Ron Howard. The reason for *Seveneves'* inclusion is that the robots in the novel are vastly different from most of the robots presented in this chapter. Considering the scientific leaning of the text, it is most likely to be quite close to reality, and in the next chapter we are closer to reality than to fiction.

The plot: The Moon breaks into seven pieces but continues to revolve around the Earth. Alas, it soon turns out that the break was not final: The pieces will continue to divide, and White Sky (a cloud of dust) and a Hard Rain (a meteorite bombardment) will depopulate the Earth. One of the solutions is to build a Cloud Ark, and send the "delegates," who will carry on the human race, in small "arklets" to join the existing International Space Station (called ISS or Izzy).

ISS is bolted to an asteroid called Amalthea, and its original function was to mine the asteroid for nickel and iron. This work was to be done by robots, programmed, run, and supervised by Dinah MacQuarie:

> … she programmed, tested, and evaluated a menagerie of robots, ranging in size from cockroach to cocker spaniel, all adapted for the task of crawling around on the surface of Amalthea, analyzing its mineral composition, cutting bits off, and taking them to a smelter. (p. 9)

> Scurrying over [the astroid's] surface was a score of different robots, belonging to four distinct "species": one that looked like a snake, one that picked its way along like a crab, one that looked like a sort of rolling geodesic dome, and another that looked like a swarm of insects. (p. 10)

> Most software developers had to write code, compile it into a program, and then run the program to see whether it was working as intended. Dinah wrote code, beamed it into the robots scurrying around on Amalthea's surface a few meters away, and stared out the window to see whether it was working. (p. 11)

---

[45] Stephenson compensates for it in Part III, which takes place 5,000 years later and is completely fictitious. (Robots start being used for rather fictitious tasks as well – making whips used in fights, for example, p. 845.)

As new problems arose (for example, a possible shortage of transistors, which could be destroyed by cosmic rays; new ones will not be sent from Earth anymore), and Dinah's and the robots' tasks had to change.

> The world's military-industrial complexes had put a lot of money and brainpower into making "rad-hard" electronics, more resistant to cosmic ray strikes. The resulting chips and circuit boards were, by and large, clunkier than the sleek consumer electronics that earthbound customers had come to expect. A lot more expensive too. So much so that Dinah had avoided using them at all in her robots. She used cheap, tiny off-the-shelf electronics in the expectation that a certain number of her robots would be found dead every week. A functional robot could carry a dead one back to the little airlock between Dinah's workshop and the pitted surface of Amalthea, and Dinah could swap its fried circuit board out for a new one. Sometimes the new one would already be dead, struck by a cosmic ray while it was just sitting there in storage. (pp. 44–45)

Thus, Dinah ordered the robots to cut a storage niche in the asteroid and hide all sensitive electronic materials there, using an eight-legged robot to insert them, but also to cover them with its body (observe that Dinah's robots could be "found dead"; very un-humanoid robots are described now and then in terms conventionally used to describe animals).

There were several types of robots. The Grabb (Grabby Crab) was the one with eight legs, made mostly of iron, with an electromagnet on its tip, which kept it on the surface of the asteroid. It was good for picking things up, during which task it switched off the magnet. A Siw (probably named after a sidewinder snake) was originally designed for exploring collapsed buildings. The electromagnets were arranged around its body in a double helix, so it could roll diagonally by switching some of them on and off. A Buckie (short for a kind of football), was bigger and spherical, so it could roll in various directions. Finally, there were nanorobots, called Nats, powered by the sun, which were supposed to work in a swarm.

At the time of the catastrophe, a mining magnate put a comet-mining spacecraft Ymir into operation, planning to bring an ice comet close to ISS, thus supplying Cloud Ark with water. He needed to borrow Dinah's robots for the task, but first they had to learn to deal with ice. In a test, one of Dinah's collaborators emptied a cardboard box full of Nats (which look like silicon beetles) on a block of ice. Some of the Nats fell on the floor, but after a while they scaled the block, joining the others, and they all began to tunnel into the ice.

Rhys, a British engineer originally sent to ISS to arrange tours for space tourists had some scientists among his ancestors whose work made him think of a new use for surplus Nats, which were bigger and less flexible than the newer models. Rhys "turned them into a new kind of robot that he dubbed the Flynk, for flying link; he taught them to be really good at forming themselves up into chain" (p. 342) that could be wrapped around various objects, so the objects could be moved when needed. (Flynk will be a great help when Ymir has to be saved later on.) Yet there were some dangers, too – a contaminated robot may spread the contamination wherever it goes. When Dina put it to work, however:

> Then she pulled up the window she used to communicate with her network of robots and typed in a single-word command: JETTISON. It was the name of a program (…) meant to be run simultaneously by every robot in the shard, as well as some other systems down in the boiler room. A prompt came back: ARE YOU SURE Y/ N Y, she typed. (…)
> Ymir had begun grumbling. Dinah felt as if she were trapped inside the belly of a frost giant with indigestion. What she was hearing, she knew, was the collective noise made by thousands of Nats, and hundreds of larger robots, as they moved to safe positions on the inner surface of the hollow shard and gnawed away at the structural webbing that connected it to the reactor core. (pp. 491–492)

At the end of the two first parts, the robots weld what remains of the ISS, arklets, and other ships in a safe position into a cleft between two asteroids.

As a movie is still in production, we avoid spoilers as much as possible, especially as the dramatic tensions of the plot do not depend on robots. Siwis, Buckies, Nats, and Grabbs (which can also be Grimmed – that is, covered with steel armor) work tirelessly for their human masters (or rather mistresses, as *Seveneves* can be seen as a depiction of a matriarchate), and when they fail, it is not their fault. Once again, the (obviously intended) animalization is worth emphasizing:

> Dinah pulled herself into position before her triptych of flat-panels, and began opening windows, checking on the activities of her menagerie of robots: some sunning themselves on the outside to soak up power, others sipping juice from the reactors, some mining propellant for the next burn, others mending the nozzle. (p. 465)

So, robots not as (humanoid) slaves, but as working animals? Taking care of well and performing tasks that humans are too weak, too big, or not skillful enough to perform?

5. Robots in popular culture: a tentative taxonomy

In order to summarize our analysis, we constructed a tentative taxonomy to answer two double-barreled questions. What good things can robots do to people and what bad things can robots do to people? What good things and what bad things can people do to robots? We intentionally chose the polysemic terms "bad" and "good" exactly because they suggest both functional and moral assessment.

In case the reader may tend to think that this taxonomy is not merely simple, but that it is simplistic, we justify our choice with a quote from Stephen Turner (2014: 138):

> ... social theory often begins with taxonomy. Taxonomies create categories of like objects that are alike in a definable way. They enable us to group things in a way that allows us to avoid the confusions produced by general terms, including of course the terms that we use in explanations of different practices, like corruption. But they also help with attempts at generalization, because new taxonomies can help us reveal commonalities within the new taxonomic category. Taxonomy is the sister of analogizing: it is a map of where to apply analogies to similar cases.

Our taxonomy contains four categories, and their content is presented in Tables 5.1 and 5.2.

Most interesting, and perhaps most surprising is the fact that the idea of "freeing people from work" vanished so quickly. Yet Burenstam Linder's *The harried leisure class* came out already in 1970; soon afterward it turned out that the leisure class not only works a great deal, but wants to work a great deal (see e.g. Schor, 1991).

In contrast, although sci-fi authors stopped writing about robots depriving people of their jobs even earlier than they stopped writing about robots providing people with leisure, this deprivation is going to be one of main themes, if not *the* main theme in media debates. The reason is partly because people want to work, and unemployment is a central topic for the economy, and therefore for politics.

Table 5.1 *What good can robots do?*

Perform all "dirty, dull and dangerous" jobs (an expression taken from GE Digital's blog): R.U.R.; Player Piano; 2001; Star Wars; Blade Runner; The Matrix; Stepford Wives; Interstellar, Seveneves
Perform jobs that are impossible for human bodies: 2001; Blade Runner; Interstellar; Seveneves
Perform complex tasks better than people can: Player Piano; 2001; Star Wars, robot-surgeon; Big Hero 6, Interstellar
Work faster and more efficiently; learn new skills more quickly: R.U.R (all later works take these two advantages as givens)
Free people from work: R.U.R., Player Piano, 2001 (but no later works)
Protect and defend people: Star Wars, good droids; Snow Crash, the dogs; Big Hero 6
Offer companionship, sympathy, and care: I, Robot; 2001; Big Hero 6
Surpass their programming: Player Piano; 2001; Star Wars, good droids; Snow Crash, the Librarian
Take over the world, as people are self-destructive: I, Robot
Help to save the world, as people are destructive: 2001; Interstellar

Table 5.2 *What bad can robots do?*

Kill or damage people in fights among groups of people: R.U.R; I, Robot; Player Piano; 2001; Big Hero 6
Commit criminal acts: R.U.R; I, Robot; Blade Runner; Big Hero 6
Deprive people of jobs: R.U.R., Player Piano
Ridicule people: Snow Crash, the Librarian; Interstellar
Surpass their programming: Player Piano; 2001; Star Wars, bad droids
Take over the world: R.U.R.; The Matrix
Use people as a source of energy: The Matrix

The first item in Table 5.3 is a typical theme for AI debates, so we shall not focus much attention on it; the second is highly topical, although not always directly discussed.

The topics in Table 5.4 are discussed primarily in philosophical terms (although it can be claimed that the idea of taxing robots belongs here – but only if one assumes that taxes are "bad").

Table 5.3 *What good people can do to robots*

Give them consciousness ("soul," "free will"): R.U.R.; I, Robot; 2001
Give them non-human shapes, making them unthreatening (remove "uncanniness") and free them from human failings: 2001; Star Wars, R2-D2; Snow Crash; Big Hero 6; Seveneves

Table 5.4   *What bad people can do to robots*

Make them human-like, and equip them with human failings: 2001; Star Wars, C-380
Use them to stop women from achieving equality: Stepford Wives
Treat robots as slaves: R.U.R.; I, Robot; Player Piano

Although we analyzed the chronology of those attributes, we could not see many particular patterns. Most authors and directors have agreed over the years that robots will perform "dirty, dull and dangerous" jobs, and that they will work and learn faster and more efficiently than the humans do. The idea of "freeing people from work" quickly faded out, as did the idea, so topical in the current media, of depriving people of work. Other topics appeared and vanished with no specific pattern that we could establish.

All in all, it seems that Karek Čapek foresaw most of the issues to be debated in the future. (Or did his groundbreaking work simply direct the future imagination?) Especially in later works, it becomes obvious that the authors and directors of works belonging to popular culture seem to realize that robots require a great deal of work. Furthermore, they do not exaggerate bad outcomes in order to achieve a dramatic effect: bad and good co-exist, but good wins (because a happy ending sells better?) Yet the authors and the directors of works in popular culture have at their disposal devices inaccessible to social scientists, and only partly accessible to journalists: They can separate bad from good by ascribing the two to different Characters, thus resolving ambiguities.

In the next chapter, we analyze the (traditional) media (although some blogs are included as well). As it is impossible to cover all the media (in all languages?), we decided to introduce a "layperson" approach. In this case, laypersons are the two of us, as we consider ourselves as having only average media interest. We may access media in more languages[1] than the average person, but as traditional media quote themselves and translate most breaking news, this does not extend our field of vision much, and it may help to illustrate general trends with some local translations.

---

[1]   English, French, German, Italian, Polish, Swedish.

6. Robotization in the media: 2014–2017

A spectre is haunting the planet—a spectre of robotization ...

Like robots themselves, the hopes and fears related to their entrance into the workplace started long before 2014. Louis Anslow (2016) helped us by summarizing what media said about robotization of work since 1920.[1]

In 1921, the *New York Times* (*NYT*) published a book review entitled "Will machines devour man?" accompanied by a picture of a person being fed into a sausage grinder. On February 26, 1928, the *NYT* published an article "March of the machine makes idle hands. Prevalence of unemployment with greatly increased industrial output points to the influence of labor-saving devices as an underlying cause."

When Albert Einstein gave a speech in Berlin in August 1930 at the opening of the Seventh German Radio and Audio Show, he "laid the world ills to machine." John Maynard Keynes shared his opinion, saying in the same year that "We are being afflicted with a new disease, 'technological unemployment.'" By 1939, everybody was using that term, although, in Anslow's opinion, employment was steadily rising. Thus, Henry Ford tried to defend the machines in the *NYT*'s World's Fair edition by writing a piece entitled "Machines as ministers to men," and predicting that machines would create more jobs than they would displace.

A year later, Massachusetts Institute of Technology (MIT) President Karl Compton and US President Franklin D. Roosevelt quarreled over the issue: The MIT president saw no problems, but Roosevelt did. Also in 1940, a US senator proposed a tax on machines, just as Bill Gates did 77 years later.

---

[1]   Although the title of his text speaks of "more than 200 years," based on a Luddite commentary from 1811, his history starts in the 1920s, with Čapek.

Pulitzer Prize winner for 1949, Hal Boyle, wrote an article called "Machines are laughing at men." (As unfolds later in this chapter, journalists were and are those most threatened by robots.)

Then in 1955 President Dwight Eisenhower called the popular fears of automation groundless. Yet the *NYT* reported in 1956 that "Automation in Britain stirs unrest in labor." And a year later, the newspaper published a balanced piece called "Promise and peril of automation."

When John F. Kennedy was elected in 1960, there were immediate appeals to him to solve the problem of technological unemployment. In 1961, the *NYT* ran an article that began: "The rise in unemployment has raised some new alarms around an old scare word: automation." What happened after that deserved the name of escalating hysteria, according to Anslow. It prompted Peter Drucker to write an article in 1965 entitled "Automation is not a villain."

There was a quiet decade or so, but at the end of the 1970s, the threat of computer chips was emerging. By the 1980s, the computer fear cycle was in full swing. The *NYT* warned in 1980: "A robot is after your job." Later, however, the topic of the threat of automation seemed to disappear from the media. Yet after the dot-com crash, positive attitudes towards technology crashed, too. And now Anslow concluded, with the promise of self-driving cars and consumers facing accumulating AI applications, "the fear of automation is once again at a fever pitch" (Anslow, 2016).

Our analysis in this chapter demonstrates that now as then, the picture is more complex than it may appear. But before we start, we need to report that the review of 175 news items, blogs, and articles in popular media revealed a certain repetitiveness. This situation occurs because media in other languages often refer to English texts (even when speaking of Japanese roboticists) and that they quote the same reports and the same scientific books that we review in Chapters 2 and 7. (In the case of scientific works, journalists often interview the authors, who are invited to give a short version of their works.) Additionally, almost all the articles or news we are quoting can be found in numerous other versions in the same language and in other languages. The media do what they are supposed to do – they mediate.

In the analysis, we primarily use the same categories that we derived from reviewing the works of science fiction, although some of them are missing, some became slightly reformulated, and others have been added. The most significant addition is the category "It is all more complicated …," a grouping that comprises media voices combining negative and positive effects of robotization, with attempts at balance.

Our classification is obviously subjective. Yet if we asked a robot for help, at present it could only count the number of words used, which is not exactly our aim. Thus, it is a discourse analysis – more in a Foucauldian spirit than in the technical meaning of Discourse Analysis.

To make reading easier, we have attached a number to each of the sources we have referenced; the complete list identifying each number is in the Appendix. The sources are ordered chronologically – the smaller the number, the earlier the source. We then present categories in order of the decreasing number of instances a given topic has been mentioned and set the new category "It is all more complicated ..." last.

6.1 WHAT ROBOTS CAN DO TO PEOPLE: GOOD

6.1.1 Perform All "Dirty, Dull, and Dangerous" Jobs (30 Instances)

In their latest book, *Machine, platform, crowd* (2017) MacAfee and Brynjolfsson added a fourth D to the dirty, dull, and dangerous jobs: "dear" jobs. But just like the alliteration itself, the idea seems rather forced and was mentioned only once (158).

The media agree on all three "Ds," but the first D: dirty – robots that do cleaning – is treated as the most obvious. The use of domestic robots is growing (13, 21, 78, 97, 99). MacAfee and Brunjolfsson's readers are informed that the Dyson 36 Eye "costs a lot, it isn't perfect, and it certainly isn't a must-buy for everyone. But it is the best robot vacuum right now." But robots can also do sewer reconnaissance (147).

As to the second D – dull jobs – there are of course varying ideas about which jobs are dull, but there is a general opinion that robots doing dull jobs will make people's lives easier (42) and less monotonous (20, 67, 78, 92, 97). There is also a list of "13 things Apple should automate after driverless cars," which comprises all boring everyday activities, including tooth brushing (153).

Although milking and livestock farming seem to be unproblematic (13, 59), a relatively new area of "dull jobs" is cooking, or at least "simple cooking." "Sally" at Casabots in Stanford makes salads, but the owners look for a celebrity chef to come with new recipes (113). There is also talk of robot butlers (118). Microrobots can perform simple medical tasks, like scraping plaque from arteries (46, 147).

The most discussed among "dull" jobs is journalism, or at least some parts of it (44). According to Associated Press, robots "will free journalists to do more journalism and less data processing" (11). Robots make less factual errors, but are unable to analyze (36). They can also "inform the readers about events that journalists never should bother about," like some local information and events (40).

Dangerous, D jobs abound (4, 12, 13, 74, 112, 115, 119, 147, 154). Humanoid robots are already working in disaster areas (4), the Da Vinci system sends robot surgeons to the frontline (12), and robots can do mine clearance (13). The Defense Advanced Research Project Agency (DARPA), which is often mentioned here, organized Robotics Challenge, a world competition for robots that can work in disaster areas, whether natural or created by humans (39). In 2015, the winner was the South Korean DRC-Hubo, which was prepared to act in situations like the one caused by Fukushima disaster (41). In 2017, the Australian roboticist Rodney Brooks (presently a professor emeritus at MIT) actually visited Fukushima, to which his iRobot company had previously sent six robots to help clean up the effects of the reactor's explosion (154).

The Italian competitor, Walk-man, lost the competition, and was degraded to doing dull jobs (55). The work on robots able to work in hazardous areas continues: Honda has built an Asimo (74), and South Korean Hankook Mirae Technology has entered the market with still newer Methods (119).

Dangers come not only from objects: Duke University School of Nursing has introduced Tele-Robotic Intelligent Nursing Assistant (Trina), which helps to limit contacts with infectious diseases (115). In general, there is an agreement that robots should do dangerous jobs. A US survey revealed that, although many opinions were split between the two parties, 85 percent of surveyed persons were of the opinion that automation should be limited to dangerous jobs (159).

6.1.2   Offer Companionship, Sympathy, and Care (18 Instances)

We expected primarily negative opinions concerning the possibility of interpersonal relations between robots and people, but we were wrong. Apparently, said Sherry Turkle from MIT (who was not pleased with this possibility at all), "Child schema and animal button eyes ... trigger an anthropomorphic reflex. (...) We perceive the machine as a creature, although we know it is only a machine. If she then shows interest in us, the Darwinian buttons are pressed" (2). It seems, indeed, that US soldiers develop emotional relationships with military robots (164).

There are human-like toys for autistic children and robo-pets for all children (14). Little Fish, produced by Baidu (Google's Chinese competitor) helps children to maintain contact with parents who work far away (117). ASIMO (Asimov gives inspiration to many robots), which is short so as not to frighten children, lectures them on the value of mathematics (74). The iCub, produced by Istituto Italiano di Tecnologia in Genua will grow from child to adult, keeping pace with its (future) owner (21).

A big area of use for robots is healthcare and care for the elderly. There is an "animatronic nurse" (12); the therapy cat, Justocat (47); and Charlie from University La Trobe, Melbourne, which helps to care for the elderly, but is not meant for children (96, 112).

Sweden and Japan are two countries facing an aging population and not enough care personnel, so both countries are interested in care robots (63). Yet the Swedish elderly are not fond of humanoid robots. Enter GiraffPlus, which provides information about old people living alone (57), and cats that can play with dementia patients (76). Cardiff Lab works with robots that are meant to care for the elderly, but also work as "a butler in the house," controlled via the Internet (46).

In fact, there are several robots in development that are supposed to keep healthy adults company: a "social robot" Jibo, developed by MIT's Cynthia Breazeal (10) and Sony's Aibo dog (88). The famous SoftBank's Pepper (operated by AI Watson, IBM's AI that won the chess tournament with a human), which is "intended to make people happy," was introduced in the UK in 2016 (88). The prediction is that Pepper will be in most Swedish households by 2026 (116).

And then there are sexbots. Turkle again: "We may actually prefer the kinship of machines to relationship with real people and animals." After all, the owner of Abyss Creations, the manufacturer of RealDoll, admits that he "doesn't really like to be around people" (65).[2]

6.1.3   Create Jobs (16 Instances)

A completely optimistic tone dominates those media that are predicting the creation of many new jobs through robotization or pointing out that many jobs are impossible to automate. Moravec's paradox is often quoted: "it is comparatively easy to make computers exhibit adult level performance on intelligence tests or playing checkers, and difficult or

---

[2]   More on this topic in Devlin (2019).

impossible to give them the skills of a one-year-old when it comes to perception and mobility" (56). Robots cannot acquire tacit knowledge (27, 54). Researchers from the Centre for European Economic Research in Mannheim claim that only 9 percent of jobs are automatable (95).

What is to be expected is a rapid growth in demand for highly skilled tasks involving regular interaction with IT, and an increase in lower-paid work, ranging from caring to hospitality, which is difficult to automate (1, 27). This observation leads to another prediction: the polarization of jobs. But it has been argued that job polarization is merely a US phenomenon, which has become unjustly generalized, and that more generally everything will be as usual – some jobs will vanish, others will appear (85). And after 200 years of concerns about automation (144), we should all be used to it by now. As Stephen Watt from Canada's University of Waterloo expressed it: "... this has been happening for decades, if not centuries, and it will continue for decades and centuries" (95).

Which jobs will be created? Nobody knows; after all nobody was able to predict the arrival of software and mobile devices in the 1900s (90, 143). In the opinion of frequently quoted David Autor, MIT, "just because we can't predict what we'll be doing, doesn't mean we'll be doing nothing" (143).

Polarization could have been caused not by outsourcing but by automation (90); robotization did help to stop the Bicycle Corporation of America from having to outsource to China and create 140 new jobs (129). It has been suggested that USA should stop outsourcing, and start constructing its own robots, rather than importing them from China (130, 137). It is to be expected that as robots become cheaper, more entrepreneurs will use them and expand their production. For this to be achieved, USA must beat China in robot production (142).

Although polarization, outsourcing, and competition with China can be seen primarily as US problems, similar developments are occurring in other countries. SKF opened a fully automated factory in Gothenburg, Sweden, and plans to do so in other countries. "But this means that outsourced production can come back, and that highly competent human personnel is needed" (141).

In general, "as machines take jobs, companies need to get creative about making new ones," says a faculty member of Singularity University (148), a Silicon Valley think tank founded, among others, by Ray Kurzweil, who launched the Singularity concept (more of which in the next chapter).

6.1.4 Perform Complex Tasks As Well or Better Than People (15 Instances)

Robots will be "reaching deep into previously protected areas of professional work like translation, medical diagnostics, the law, accountancy, even surgery" (1). And they will do these jobs "not necessarily the same way people do, i.e. by imitating them. Professions like healthcare, law, education, audit, tax, consulting, journalism, architecture and divinity[3] transform in ways opening the doors for robots, and making them welcome" (108). It seems that robots will learn to create not by imitating humans, but by learning from creative works[4] (114), easily producing fact books and encyclopedias (122).

Robots are good at large-scale data processing (67) and are therefore able to make cancer diagnoses at early stages (114). Ginni Rometty from IBM claimed that a robot operated by AI Watson would soon be "the best oncologist in the world" (96, 125). Brynjolfsson admitted being wrong about "three human skills" (complex perception and manipulation, creative intelligence, and social intelligence); it turns out that robots are excellent at pattern recognition in large data sets (95). Not only they can diagnose; they can also assist surgeons, whose arms age quicker than their brains (12, 13).

In contrast to critics concerned with the fate of professionals (which we will list later), many of the more optimistic voices note that robotization will help democracy, rendering public tenders truly objective, for example (96). Hassabis, the founder of DeepMind Technologies, has suggested that automated financial advice would be affordable to anyone (114, 96); McAfee agreed (138), adding that the same could be said of basic healthcare.

Somewhat unexpectedly, many people believe that robots can be better bosses than people (173). *Star Wars*' enthusiasts claim that real robots can presently do everything that the movie's robots do (175).

---

[3] Apparently, the Vatican has approved an app called "Confession" (108).

[4] Again, a Russian robot allegedly wrote a new version of *Anna Karenina* titled *True Love*. But it is correct that Ai-Da, the humanoid robot artists, can draw and paint. (https://uk.reuters.com/article/uk-tech-robot-artist/ai-da-the-humanoid -robot-artist-gears-up-for-first-solo-exhibition-idUKKCN1T61Z1, accessed June 6, 2019).

The next category is closely related to this one – the performance of complex tasks. The stress is not on complexity, however, but on speed and efficiency.

6.1.5   Work Faster and More Efficiently; Learn New Skills More Quickly (15 Instances)

Because of these capacities, the use of robots is especially visible in the four areas in which 75 percent of industrial robots work: computer and electronic goods, home appliances and components, transportation equipment, and machinery (87). Among those four, only home use is relatively new. At any rate, competition, especially from Asia, requires robotization (59). Furthermore, the changes in transportation should make city life easier and more fun by 2030 (110), whereas production will be safer, as robots are more careful than humans and avoid accidents (169).

The work of perfecting robots' speed and efficiency continues. Robot Baxter, created by Rodney Brooks, learns physical movement by imitation (2). There are trials of organic robots with flexible actuators (the units that provide movement) that can learn many types of movement (101). Robotization means that knowledge can be truly distributed, according to Gill A. Pratt from the Defense Advanced Research Projects Agency (DARPA) (54). Robots will be also capable of "fluid intelligence" (139).

Specialized robots continue to be produced. Fastbricks Robotics' Hadrian builds houses from 3D templates, creating more affordable housing for the general public (125). In fact, Robot Panda won the German Future Prize in 2017 because it can be used by anybody, and it is "safe, has exceptionally fine motor skills and is designed to collaborate with humans" (166). "Robot doctor" in China passed the general practitioners' qualifying exam, attaining 456 points out of 600 (a pass requires 360), although it is meant only as an assistant to human physicians (165).

Such comforting comments are typical when presenting robots entering highly skilled jobs, such as journalism. Narrative Science analyzes financial data, but only from a mathematical perspective (19). A German company, Aexea Interactive, uses "robotic journalism," on the grounds that it produces fewer factual mistakes (43). Chinese robot reporter Xiao Nan writes a story in a second, but it is predicted that "robots will be able to act as a supplement, helping newspapers and related media as well as editors and reporters" (126). And, finally, robots cook, but only according to recipes (37).

6.1.6 Perform Jobs that Are Impossible for Human Bodies (11 Instances)

Probably the least questionable issue surrounding robotization is the idea that robots can do things that human bodies cannot – for varying reasons. The most obvious job is that of exploring other planets, for which there are a great many robots, known as Mars Exploration Rovers, produced in many countries (70, 112). Drone robots have many uses in the construction industry. They are "useful in repairing inaccessible damaged regions of the home or other structure" (14), and, as mentioned, they can print 3D houses (145). Q-bots are also mapping old houses for which the original plans have been lost (18). In general, they are useful high in the air for delivering packages (132), and deep in the water for undertaking such tasks as cleaning up shipwrecks in Sweden (163).

Robots can also do things that are possible for human bodies in principle, but not always in practice. They can function as external skeletons, and as sophisticated prostheses (56). Because they never tire (59), Margaret Atwood came with an idea that was later realized in the form of LongPen – a robotic arm for remote book signings (18). They can also simulate human bodies – and not only human; there are robot plants and robot animals that permit unique studies of the species (66).

It is also in this context that Moravec's paradox, or at least the first part of it, is evoked: "tasks that are tough for humans … are easy for robots" (56).

6.1.7 Free People from (Boring, Low-Paid) Work (11 Instances)

This issue is more problematic, as much depends on the way the expression "free from work" is interpreted. Dutch historian Rutger Bregman propagates a "utopia for realists": "I believe in a future where jobs are for robots and life is for people" (144). There are several historical parallels: Eric Brynjolfsson imagined a "digital Athens," in which people will do important jobs, and economist Jeremy Rifkin spoke of a new Marx-like utopia of "collaborative commons"[5] (16).

Several generally positive views on this matter end with a caveat: only if there were a basic income (83); only if universities would offer

---

[5] It needs to be added that *The New York Review of Books'* reviewer, Sue Halpern, saw his view as "illusory and misleading" (16).

education "of an intrinsic value," which teaches students how to learn (95); only if governments "overhaul education systems to help a nation's people to race with the machines, instead of against them" (McAfee, 138).

Although there are voices that do not agree with the necessity of a basic income, there are other voices raising questions like "What will be the source of the money to pay for basic income?" (8). Some people suggest that the money will be raised through social media (53), but Gill A. Pratt from DARPA has suggested another solution: Everybody will have their own robot or robots, and people will make money selling their preferences (53).

6.1.8   Protect and Defend People (10 Instances)

Armies, police and fire services, and security firms can all make use of robots that can protect and defend (112, 132). The Pentagon spoke of "conversion of the US military into an army consisting to a large extent of robots, including fighting ones" (2). Some of these robots are dog-like, like in Stephenson's *Snow Crash* (2) and Boston Dynamics' Big Dog (121). Like in Stephenson's *Seveneves*, the US military has swarming drones, and an autonomous drone, Perdix, has been developed at MIT (121). The Pentagon came also with Lethal Autonomous Weapon Systems, which caused protests from scientists (127), but the Pentagon defended it, saying that "robots are not cruel" (51).

The first robot police officer was in Dubai (149, 150), but when Dallas police used a bomb-disposal robot, the legal experts were worried that it would create a grey area of use of deadly force as a means of law enforcement. Police chief answered: "We saw no other option" (93).

Robots hold great promise for security services, as they can master and remember face and body shape recognition (112, 118, 121, 125, 132).

6.1.9   Solve the World's Problems, as People Aren't Able to Do It Themselves

The most optimistic voices claim that robots will be able "to solve all our problems, famine, illnesses, homelessness, global warming" (112). This is the opinion of Demis Hassabis, previously Google's employee, now the founder of its main competitor DeepMind. DeepMind's motto is "Solve intelligence, use it to make the world a better place" (125).

Max Tegmark, a Swede now working in the Future of Life Institute in the USA, asked provocatively, what is wrong with being controlled by a superior intelligence? To think so is a sign of "carbon chauvinism" – the assumption that life requires carbon (171).

In the meantime, New Zealand claims to have constructed its first robot politician: Sam. Unlike human politicians, Sam is able to listen to everybody and make impartial decisions (172).

All in all, the positive voices about robots are more numerous than the negative ones (130 versus 89; the number does not add to 175, because some articles or blogs contain both opinions). Yet the negative voices are substantial.

6.2   WHAT ROBOTS CAN DO TO PEOPLE: BAD

6.2.1   Deprive People of Jobs (32 Instances)

This is, of course, the typical negative message. It can take a shape of a general dystopic prediction, more detailed predictions, and the list of jobs most threatened.

In the first subcategory, general predictions, the message is "Be afraid! The march of the machines is eating into our jobs, pay raises and children's prospects" (1). The transition is rapid, and therefore shocking. The "recovery, reemployment, reskilling, retraining" do not happen fast enough, according to McAfee (3) and cannot keep pace with the jobs lost. And it needs to be remembered, that "work is not just a means for distributing purchasing power. It is also among the most important sources of identity and purpose in individuals' lives" (105). Carl Benedict Frey, a Swedish researcher working at Oxford, is quite sure that "AI will butcher the job market" (although Sweden may prove somewhat more resilient, 168). And even before it happens, both threat and reality "are having adverse effects on physical health and mental wellbeing across a range of occupations," The transition will be "dramatic and painful" (160). Among other events, Brexit will trigger a "robot revolution" (120).

With respect to the second category of job loss predictions aimed at specific jobs, robots could replace 80 percent of them – low skill, low wage, to be sure, but also middle skilled and middle wage in USA (5). Moshe Verdi from Rice University has predicted 50 percent unemployment if politicians do nothing (73). In China, FoxConn, the world's tenth largest employer, has already replaced 60,000 workers with robots (125). Amazon supermarkets are said to operate with only three humans, although Amazon denies that this is so (131). The Future of Humanity Institute at Oxford asked 352 experts, most of whom were convinced that all jobs will be automated in 120 years (152). Forrester Market Research predicted that by 2021, 6 percent of all jobs in the USA would be automated, especially in the areas of transportation, logistics, customer service, and such consumer services as call centers, taxi drivers, and truckers (104).

A great many voices were raised in concern over the future of specific occupations and professions. There was a pessimistic reading of polarization: Jobs in the middle would vanish; top jobs and low-level jobs would grow (34); and both middle jobs and the middle class will vanish (118). Polarization will concern not only people, but also countries. What is more, it should be obvious that "it is better to own a robot than to work with a robot," said UBS Group economist Lutfey Siddiqui (72).

As to specific occupations, cooks are among those who should fear robots (2, 4), as robots already make pizzas (113). Call center personnel will vanish (96, 104), but so will lawyers (2, 4, 61, 92, 95). Traders and brokers will no longer be needed (29, 95), but their loss may place those who can afford a robot in a favorable trading position (81). Jeffrey Sachs and other researchers predicted that even programming will suffer from stagnation as a consequence of an economic boom ("The robots are coming for your paycheck," 24). Physicians and nurses will be replaced (2, 4, 61, 92). Scientists and university lecturers will share their fate (61, 92); in general, the definitions of "creative" and "routine" jobs will have to change (95). Add to this the fact that the new generation of bosses is extremely positive toward automation (31), and it is easy to believe Martin Ford, who was quoted as saying, "no job is safe."

Special attention has been paid to journalism (4, 36, 43, 45). Narrative Science (36, 45) has been joined by Wordsmith, which can produce number-based news about finance, sports, and weather (45). Journalists will end up like Chaplin in *Modern Times* (43) unless they mobilize their last defenses: wit and surrealism (38). Yet robots are predicted to replace entertainers too (61).

What to do? The US commentators thought that one should remember the words of Abraham Lincoln: "As our case is new, so we must think anew, and act anew" (5). Still, it could be "a difficult transition rather than a sharp break with the history," according to James Bessen, an economist at the Boston University School of Law. People fear self-driving cars like they once feared cars replacing horses. As to the fear of losing jobs, "companies and governments will need to make it easier for workers to acquire new skills and switch jobs as needed" (90).

Yet, as dramatic as it sounds, job deprivation is not the worst thing that robots can do to people.

6.2.2   Take Over the World (23 Instances)

Stephen Hawking and others depicted a future world in which robots are "outsmarting financial markets, out-inventing human researchers, out-manipulating human leaders, and developing weapons we cannot even understand" (7, 17). There could arise "distributed autonomous corporations" with no human owners, running the market (28).

Boström was speaking of "superintelligence" (8, 84, 112) in his book of the same name, but in a later interview, he suggested that such intelligences will be many: Multipolar Outcomes fighting for advantage (52). But it is Ray Kurzweil's notion of Singularity (16) that dominates the comments. According to Israeli historian Yuval Noah Harari (*Homo deus: A brief history of tomorrow*), it will be an intelligence decoupled from consciousness (30). According to Kurzweil, people need to develop their intelligence to keep up with AI (112). The DeepMind group started an AI Safety Group to foresee and defend people from Singularity-like AI. But Elon Musk does not trust them, and said that they were the only ones he feared (125). Others have stressed that AI should be regulated (15, 17). In the meantime, the SoftBank's CEO claims that his company works toward achieving Singularity (162).

What is actually happening? "A robot has passed a self-awareness test. Next step world domination" (49). There are attempts at robotic brain emulation, observed Robin Hansson, the author of *The age of em* (111). And although Sophia the robot was granted citizenship by the Kingdom of Saudi Arabia, a professor from UNSW-Canberra raised "three concerns," the most serious of which was the right to reproduce: Robots "can easily exceed the human population of a nation" (161). It has also been suggested that robots can acquire consciousness without people knowing it, especially as people do not really know what consciousness is (75).

If this sounds like science fiction,[6] it needs to be mentioned that some commentators believe the world is on its way to the situation presented

---

[6]   Media are not alone in this perception: As described in the next chapter, scientific works also liken science fiction more and more.

in *Avengers: Age of ultron* (32) and that Asimov's laws are obsolete in the face of Singularity (124), much as his dystopian predictions all come true (135). *Die Welt* took a humorous approach: "It will be a wonderful world: credible, safe, beautiful, intelligent and delicious. At least for the machines" (71). And machines that think and feel will not have much respect for humans (77).

There are also predictions of humans exploiting superintelligence, the most likely scenario being that "robots will indeed subjugate the mass of the population, but at the behest of a narrow elite of human masters" – robots will kill democracy (91). So, "let normal people beware of AI researchers" (77).

6.2.3   Cause Damage by Faulty Performance (9 Instances)

As we have demonstrated, many commentators praise robots' skills and capabilities. How about making errors, though? Robots can cause an atomic war attack by wrongly reading important signals (8) or by misunderstanding a command (136). The usual question in this context is about responsibility (6, 10, 33, 35). Who is responsible when a self-driving car causes an accident (6)? If a surgeon assistant makes a mistake (12)? If an accident is caused by following a GPS or, as has happened in flight accidents, by leaving controls to the autopilot (22)? Another often-quoted incident is that of the security robot at Stanford Shopping Center in Palo Alto that ran over and injured a toddler (98).

6.2.4   Make People Lose Some of Their Capacities (7 Instances)

It could also happen that people would trust robots too much and become less attentive, as GPS and autopilot incidents suggest (69, 112). As human trust in robots increases, people could, for instance, lose their navigation skills (22, 26, 135), which will lead to a "human impotence" (135) or even dementia (22).

People may start imitating robots at work in order to keep their jobs (103). And according to Sherry Turkle, children's relationships with smart toys will crowd out those with friends and family (167). These developments, like the ones described next, were not present in the popular cultural works that we analyzed.

6.2.5   Interfere with What People Are Doing (7 Instances)

At the extreme, there can be a "robot smog": People's machines will invade each other's personal space (1). Although this may happen in the distant future, San Francisco has already restricted the use of delivery robots (they have to produce such safety equipment as warning noises and headlights), which were found to interfere with pedestrians (151). Furthermore, robots observing people will mean that there will be even less privacy; surveillance cameras at least remain in one place (10).

There were quite a few media mentions of "creepiness," quoting examples of intrusive robotic products (16). This problem intensifies in many countries with a visibly aging population. Swedish patients and nurses do not want robots, but there are severe personnel shortages (47), so that robots are practically forced on the elderly (25). An Australian commentary concluded that robots interfering with people's actions is creepy, but it also contained a picture of a robotic Santa Claus with a robotic reindeer … (125).

6.2.6   Commit Criminal Acts (5 Instances)

Robots can commit crimes either when they are owned by people with evil intentions (136) or when they are hijacked by hackers, even for fun (10, 16). Indeed, danger lies not with Singularity, but with human criminals taking over the markets or the military, for instance. (35). It has been suggested, in fact, that Brexit voters were conned by online bots (91).

6.2.7   Kill or Damage People in Fights Among Groups of People (4 Instances)

As the Pentagon works on developing robots that can choose and eliminate their own targets, UN and Human Rights Watch wants to forbid it (7), arguing that such robots can kill people under the pretense of "defense" (9). Thus the 123 nations participating in the 2016 Convention on Certain Conventional Weapons voted to examine the possibility of banning autonomous robots that can select targets without human control (125). In the meantime, it has become known that North Korea's Hwasong-15 can reach USA (170).

6.2.8   Surpass Their Programming and Do Strange Things (2 Instances)

Apparently, a robot escaped from the Russian company, Promobot (89, 125) and "died" on the street when its battery died (89). It has been suggested, though, that the designers left the doors open twice, hoping to produce a public relations coup (125). Google Translator, however, "came out with a new way of learning – all on its own" (125).

6.3   WHAT PEOPLE CAN DO TO ROBOTS: GOOD

6.3.1   Give Them (Consciousness) Human Traits and Privileges (16 Instances)

One of good things that people can do for robots is to give them consciousness, but consciousness may appear by itself. Robots should acquire all human rights, including voting (112). It is unclear whether Sophia has consciousness, but she has become a citizen, and her example led some people to believe that, in order to help people, robots must have, like her, "mobility, dexterity, and autonomous perception" (162). Less dramatic solutions are being proposed by the EU, with a draft of "electronic personhood" – analogous to corporate personhood – to ensure the rights and responsibilities of robots (123). Luciano Floridi has suggested that it should be based on the Roman law for slaves (134).

London School of Economics researchers referred to Stanley Milgram's[7] less well-known research on "cyranoids": chatbots speaking through humans. But "if a machine can mimic physical and behavioural dimensions of us, then why wouldn't we call that human?" (50).

The most common suggestion, however, is that of instilling moral values in robots, rendering them "moral machines" (8, 9, 48, 58, 80, 82, 106, 161). One could first make an ethical evaluation of every type of robot being produced (25). British Standards Institution produced official guidelines relating to robots. "It should be possible to find out who is responsible for any robot and its behavior" (106). Then, one could start with programming in Asimov's three laws of robotics (it has been

---

[7]   US social psychologist Stanley Milgram was famous (infamous to some) for his experiments on obedience (https://en.wikipedia.org/wiki/Stanley _Milgram, accessed September 3, 2018).

noted that Asimov's story from 1942 takes place in 2015), and then teach robots ethical decision-making (48). But Asimov's laws do not seem to be enough, and there are several research places, like University of West England (UWE) in Bristol, that are working on a new, adequate ethical code (80). The Engineering and Physical Sciences Research Council (EPRSC) produced five Principles of Robotics (82), and the Future of Life Institute came up with 23 principles known as Asilomar AI Principles (161).

More practice-oriented suggestions have been advanced: to teach robots to differentiate between "right" and "wrong" orders (felicity conditions) and to trust their human collaborators (136). The suggestions amount to nothing more than teaching robots to collaborate and assist humans at work (107).

6.3.2   Make Them Unthreatening (Remove "Uncanniness") (8 Instances)

EPRSC's fourth Principle of Robotics says that robots "should not be designed in a deceptive way to exploit vulnerable users; instead their machine nature should be transparent" (82) – an opinion with which many people agree (80, 81). The ways of achieving this goal are varied. Some people think that uncanniness can be removed by simply giving robots a smile and gentle features (112). Others think that robots should be humanoid but not too realistic (23) – perhaps like the children's robot, Cozmo (167). (Swedish researchers collected popular stories about "Caring Monsters" to find inspiration there (47)). At least one Japanese robot maker considered *Star Wars*' R2-D2 an ideal model (88).

6.4   WHAT PEOPLE CAN DO TO ROBOTS: BAD

6.4.1   Make Them Human-Like, and Equip Them with Human Failings, or Make Them Provoke Human Failings (6 Instances)

Microsoft AI Tay got itself a Twitter account and soon reproduced the worst hate messages imaginable (79, 86, 114). An experiment that made HAL (from *2001*) speak to Samantha (from *Her*), revealed that "men, even male-defined AI, are real assholes" (100). Furthermore, "it's difficult to listen to, because it is entirely human" (100). According to Professor of Robotics Alan Winfield, from UWE Bristol, "To design a gendered robot is a deception," as it provokes gender-cued responses and sexism (80). The journalists watching "Professor Einstein" (produced by Hanson Robotics) decided that even if it was too small to decrease uncanniness, it was creepy (128). As Margaret Atwood has commented, in this respect, real life gets closer to fiction (18).

6.4.2   Treat Robots as Slaves (2 Instances)

At least two authors have mentioned robots as slaves. Luciano Floridi has suggested that Roman laws for slaves should be a model for constructing an electronic personhood (134), and Eric Brynjolfsson advanced the idea of a "digital Athens," in which people will do really important jobs, like Greek men did (2).

6.4.3   Make Robots that Can Hurt People (1 Instance)

The notion of robots that could cause physical harm to people is a truly exceptional idea, but the engineer Alexander Reben, an MIT-trained artist and roboticist, did it "just for fun" (125). But other amateurs are designing "defense robots," while the professionals in South Korea, Germany, Israel, and of course the Pentagon are designing autonomous killer robots, ostensibly for legitimate defense only.

6.5   "IT IS ALL MORE COMPLICATED …"

Both McAfee and Brynjolfsson believe that what people are presently witnessing is but another industrial revolution – this time in the form of digital transformation. It may be difficult, they admit, but suggest that it will end in full employment (3, 22). Others agree that "the real robot invasion won't be a dramatic humanoid uprising. But it will be extremely profitable" (174). In his *Utopia for Realists*, Rutger Bregman put it less elegantly: "Anybody who fears mass unemployment underestimates capitalism's extraordinary ability to create new bullshit jobs" (although it will end with the introduction of basic income, 144).

So, from where come the dystopian images? After all, technology development is not like natural evolution; yet it is presented in fatalistic ways, with Darwinian analogies (32). Technological progress is not deterministic (56). According to one Swedish teacher of robotics, AI researchers exaggerate in order to attract attention and funds (32, but see 68). Similarly, the US Department of Defense considers the alleged development of Artificial General Intelligence (AGI) by the DeepMind company extremely unlikely to happen, yet it receives a great deal of attention. Furthermore, there are cultural differences in perceiving robot revolution, which are usually ignored; for example, 60 percent of surveyed Germans wanted to ban armed drones and robots in wars, whereas 70 percent of US citizens wanted them used (157).

What did the actual predictions look like? They varied, sometimes dramatically. The Centre for European Research calculated that 42 percent of German workers will lose their jobs to robots; OECD gave it 12 percent (146). One source listed eight industries that robots will completely transform by 2025: "predictions that are interesting – and sometimes scary" (64). Predictions of labor shortages in the USA are actually getting worse, because there are many sectors that cannot be fully automated and will require people with high-level skills working with machines – and there are not many such people (94). According to the World Economic Forum, 5 million jobs will be lost by 2020, and 2.1 million will be created – jobs that will require workers who "successfully combine mathematical and interpersonal skills" (102). Robots, in the meantime, will learn such human traits as sympathy, moral judgment, and dexterity (95).

In Canada, there is a fear of job-stealing, career-crushing robots, which will happen in the USA in 50–100 years. According to Frank Pasquale from University of Maryland, both predictions are right and wrong: he took a "middle-ground view" (140). The CEO of Deutsche Bank said: "In our bank we have people doing work like robots. Tomorrow we will have robots behaving like people." They may employ fewer accountants, but those who are left will be doing meaningful work (155). There are some US predictions that the loss of jobs will mainly affect one group: moderately educated men – thus Trump's election victory (146).

And then there is Rodney Brooks again, with "The Seven Deadly Sins of Predicting the Future of AI." "Predicting the future is really hard, especially ahead of time"; yet there are four general topic or areas where faulty predictions usually appear:

1. AGI: possible in principle, but far away …
2. Singularity: another couple of centuries, if at all? (the nonsense of exponentialism)
3. Misaligned values between humans and machines. Do horses share human values?

4.   Really Evil AI is propagated primarily by Hollywood science
       fiction (156).

Well, according to Google's Research Center in Zurich, in the best cases
a robot's intelligence (Sophia included) equals that of a worm (164). At
the same time SoftBank's CEO believes that in next 30 years there will
be robots with an IQ of 10,000 (162).

Some voices sounded resigned: Calun Chace, the author of *The economic singularity* said that "Homo Sapiens will be split into a handful
of gods and the rest of us" (60). As Hawking said, whatever happens,
it should be carefully studied (109), and Boström agreed (118). And as
Bill Gates suggested, robots will take over jobs, so introduce robot taxes
(133, 134).

Interestingly enough, only two voices raised a question that seems
central to us: the question of energy. As one source stated, nobody knows
whose consciousness prediction will be right, but does anybody know
how to solve the energy problem? (62) As Margaret Atwood put it, robotics needs energy: Where do we get it from? (18)

And so it continues, but at a slower pace, it seems to us, as there are
other things to report – global warming among others. Here are some
examples: In 2018, *The Atlantic* reported that robots would transform
the production and sale of fast food, and "that might not be a bad thing."[8]
The journalists from the magazine of Swedish university teachers' union
visited Hiroshi Ishiguro, who made a Geminoid robot that looks like him.[9]
In April 2018, the robotics experts told the European Parliament that its
civil-law rules of robotics are based mostly on science fiction.[10] The
robotists at Nanyang Technological University in Singapore have taught
two robots to assemble an IKEA chair.[11] Relatively new is the accusation
formulated by Gilberto Corbellini in *Il Sole 24 Ore*[12]: he believes that
intellectuals (especially humanists) are suffering from technophobia. The
rest of the article glorifies the uses of robots in medicine. *Wall Street
Journal*, however, delivered a "postmortem" on IBM's Watson, and other

---

[8]   https://www.theatlantic.com/magazine/archive/2018/01/iron-chefs/
546581/, accessed June 20, 2018.
[9]   *Universitetsläraren* nr 3, 2018, 30–33.
[10]   https://www.irishtimes.com/business/technology/robotics-experts-tell-eu
-to-stop-relying-on-science-fiction-1.3473913, accessed June 20, 2018.
[11]   *Dagens Nyheter*, April 22, 2018.
[12]   "Se il robot è meglio del medico," *Il Sole 24 Ore*, July 8, 2018: 23.

media joined in, accusing IBM of "overhyping" its capacity to diagnose cancer.[13] In general, however, the hype seems to have subsided, although the May 3, 2019 edition of Sweden's *Dagens Nyheter* returned to SKF, a Swedish ball-bearing factory, now a global corporation, as they did two years ago (85), but this time claiming that the company will soon cut its workforce in half because of its ongoing robotization. On the same day, the other Swedish daily, *Svenska Dagbladet*, published a *démenti* from Amazon, in which the giant denied the rumor that it is going to replace its employees with robots. The same daily reported on June 8, 2019 that the roboticists from the Royal Institute of Technology in Stockholm built a robot called Tengai that can be used in recruitment interviews.

Unless something dramatic happens, robot news will be trickling down at a steady pace. So now it is time to leave this middle ground to see what the social scientists have to say.

---

[13] https://slate.com/business/2018/08/ibms-watson-how-the-ai-project-to -improve-cancer-treatment-went-wrong.html, accessed August 23, 2018.

7.   Robotization in social sciences

> The time is ripe for a more comprehensive overview that will balance the
> pessimistic with the optimistic, the technophobe with the technophile, the war-
> monger with the industrial designer, the literary intellectual with the inventor.
> (Bowler, 2017: 4)

7.1   SOME PREMONITIONS FROM THE PAST

Although the main focus of our analysis has been directed toward social
scientists writing about robotization in the 2010s, it must be noted that
certain topics return over time. This is why we begin with observations
made by historian of futurology Peter J. Bowler (2017).

7.1.2   Prophets of Progress

Like us, Bowler emphasized that science fiction, popular science, and
science and technology were connected in a circle of mutual influences
throughout the past century. Scientists wrote novels and sent articles
to the media ("Asimov had a PhD in chemistry, worked at the Naval
Experimental Station and went on to teach biochemistry at Boston
University School of Medicine," Bowler, 2017: 28.) The idea that robots
will be doing actual work and not merely on the theater stage existed
early on. Bowler quoted engineer and physicist Archibald Montgomery
Low's book, *Our wonderful world of tomorrow* (1934), which contained
a chapter entitled "The robot age." The robots he described were mostly
industrial workers, but more options were to arise in print. In 1954, in
his novel, *The caves of steel*, Asimov introduced a New York detective
working with a robot colleague. And in the 1960s, Herman Kahn and
Anthony J. Wiener assumed that households would be run by robots by
2000.

Have these prophecies become true? As one might have guessed,
"[t]he modern world has seen some of these predictions fulfilled, while
others seem increasingly wide of the mark" (Bowler, 2017: 81).

7.1.2   Facts, Fiction, and Prediction

In Jasia Reichardt's 1978 book, briefly mentioned in Chapter 3, the author introduced issues that are still being discussed today:

> ... whether in literature or in the real world, robots are used for fighting wars, protecting property, enforcing law, or taking responsibility for human beings; even if it is entirely for their own good, there is an implicit danger. The danger is based on two main factors. The first has to do with the fact that if you have rules, you must have exceptions to those rules, and to date machines have no conception of such an idea. Exceptions are by definition unforeseeable (…)
> The second, and even more basic factor is biological altruism which must constitute a part of the make-up of a responsible robot, if man is to survive (…) (p. 118)

She has supported her reasoning by quoting from Norbert Wiener's (1960) book, *The brain and the machine*:

> There is nothing which will automatically make the automatic factory work for human good, unless we have determined this human good in advance and have so constructed the factory as to contribute to it. If our sole orders to the factory are for an increase in production, without regard to the problems of unemployment and of the distribution of human labour, there is no self-working principle of *laissez-faire* which will make those orders redound to our benefit and even prevent them from contributing to our own destruction. The responsibilities of automation are new, profound, and difficult. (111–112; in Reichardt, 1978: 144)

It turns out that the whole field of control and communication theory that Wiener called "cybernetics" has been used since at least 1838; it means "governance." (*Gubernatio* was a Latin corruption of the Greek word *kubernetes*, a steerman.)

The last chapters of her book, richly illustrated with various pictures of robots, contain a discussion about artificial intelligence: "the science of making machines do things that would require intelligence if done by men" (after Minsky, 1966) and consciousness – again, the same issues that are being currently discussed (superintelligence, robot rights, etc.).

In the very last chapter, Reichardt attempted to predict the future, saying at the start that such predictions are usually wrong. She was right in that she was wrong. She did not think there would be any use for robots in the home, and in medicine robots would be "receptionists and interviewers."

7.1.3   The Contemporary History of Cybernetics

Although the 1980s are known as the winter season for AI and related
issues, the interest (and, most likely, the money) were starting to return
in the 1990s. In 1994, Katherine N. Hayles, a professor of literature with
a strong interest in technology, presented an analysis of three waves in
the development of cybernetics. Her main focus was on the first wave,
from 1945 to 1960, and her material constituted transcripts from a series
of conferences sponsored by the Josiah Macy Foundation that took place
from 1946 to 1953.

The seventh and eighth conferences (1951 and 1952) were dedicated
primarily to a discussion of Shannon's "electronic rat," as he called
his maze-solving device. Everybody agreed that it was an amazing
invention, but Heinz von Foerster, Margaret Mead, and Hans Teuber
emphasized that "We all know that we ought to study the organism, and
not the computers, if we wish to understand the organism. Differences
in levels of organization may be more than quantitative" (after Hayles,
1994: 453). Hayles was even more explicit: "By suggesting certain kinds
of experiments, the analogues between intelligent machines and humans
construct the human in terms of the machine" (Hayles, 1994: 453).

The first wave launched the idea of homeostasis, based on the assumption that all living systems are always trying to reach it, rendering it easy
to reproduce in the form of machines. With time, noticed Hayles, this
assumption was more and more disrupted by the idea of reflexivity.

> If what is exactly stated can be done by a machine, the residue of the uniquely
> human becomes coextensive with the qualities of language that interfere with
> precise specification – its ambiguity, metaphoric play, multiple encoding, and
> allusive exchanges between one symbol system and another. (…) This train of
> thought indicates how the rival constellations of homeostasis and reflexivity
> assimilated other elements into themselves. On the side of homeostasis was
> instrumental language, while ambiguity, allusion, and metaphor stood with
> reflexivity. (Hayles, 1994: 456)

Those who were on the side of homeostasis believed that humans are
mechanisms that respond to their environments by trying to maintain
homeostasis, that the function of scientific language is exact specifica-
tion, that intelligent machines simply require exactly formulated problems, and that exactness is more important than meaning.

Those who were on the side of reflexivity protested that people cannot
be seen as input/output devices in which the internal psychological com-

plexity is treated as a black box. Their antagonists feared that such concepts as "internal psychological complexity" meant that "science slips into subjectivity" (p. 459), which a real science must not do. The way out of this conflict was offered by Maturana's epistemology of autopoiesis,[1] which showed that perception is species specific, and that there is, therefore, no perspective from which to see reality as "it really is." Maturana's model was accepted even by those who opted for "objective science," because he never pointed out that also this model was but a product of human perception.

As Hayles summarized the development of cybernetics:

> ... the field is moving along a trajectory that arcs from homeostasis to reflexivity to emergence/immersion. First stability is privileged; then a system's ability to take as its goal the maintenance of its own organization; then its ability to manifest emergent and unpredictable properties (...) that evolve spontaneously through feedback loops between human and machine.
>
> The larger narrative inscribed here thus locates the subject in the changing relation to intelligent machines that points towards looming transformation: the era of the human is about to give way, or has already given way, to the posthuman.
>
> Howard Rheingold has called it IA, intelligence augmentation, arguing that humans and intelligent machines are entering into a symbiosis to which each will bring the talents and gifts specific to their species: humans will contribute to the partnership pattern recognition, language capability, and understanding ambiguities; machines will contribute rapid calculation, massive memory storage, and rapid data retrieval. (Hayles, 1994: 466–467)

Collaborative robots – cobots – were invented two years after the publication of Hayles' article.[2]

7.1.4 Humanoids in the 2000s

In 2003, Swedish roboticist Peter Nordin wrote a book with journalist Johanna Wilde that was intended as an easy introduction to robotics. Throughout the entire book, Nordin expressed his belief that robots will play a significant role not so much (or not more than before) in industry as in entertainment. (The robots he constructed at Chalmers Technical University in Gothenburg were called Elvis and Priscilla.)

---

[1] She quotes the famous article "What the frog's eye tells the frog's brain," https://hearingbrain.org/docs/letvin_ieee_1959.pdf.

[2] https://patents.google.com/patent/US5952796, accessed May 7, 2019.

He drew an analogy with the 1400s, when the first dramatic invention was paper, then the press. We now have computers. "Today we have cheap systems for handling information – cheap computers – but we don't have an effective way to program them mechanically" (Nordin and Wilde, 2003: 5). We have paper; now we need a press.

He also posted a question about why do so many people study and develop only humanoids. His answer was as follows:

> To begin with, it is an excellent way to demonstrate what AI is. (...) A small robot that learns how to go is an example that everybody can understand. Humanoids are therefore excellent devices to fulfil university's "third task," that is, public outreach (...)
>
> Another reason is that construction of humanoids is an ideal method for testing the integration of different AI-techniques. (...)
>
> The third reason to work with humanoid robots is a belief that they will become commercially very important. (...) humanoid industry can become as big as car industry, if not bigger. (...)
>
> Today we are discovering yet another important reason to use exactly the humanoids: our need to mirror ourselves. We people identify us more with a machine that looks like us, and therefore find it easier to communicate with it, for example via body language. (...) The aim [of the entertainment and experience industry] is to provoke emotions in the participants, and no matter what emotions they should be, a humanoid is the most engaging type of robot. A robot that looks like a person is perceived as more frightening, funny, pitiful, sexy, nice, irritating, amusing, sad, thought-provoking, manipulative or crazy than a robot that looks like a household machine. (Nordin and Wilde, 2003: 30, translation BC)

He evoked the example of Japanese roboticists, who do not shy away from humanoids, and attempted to explain why. We return to this topic in greater detail later in this chapter.

Nordin presented a short history of robotics, beginning with John McCarthy and continued with Marvin Minsky, Alan Turing, Hugh Loebner, and other roboticists. Industry robots represented the first use of robots, and their mass production started in the 1960s. But it was not until 1967 that robots were able to walk.

According to Nordin, there is more research on humanoids in USA than in Europe, but he suggests that could be because US roboticists are leading the AI research. He quoted Rodney Brook, who was also convinced that "it is impossible to be intelligent without a body" (Nordin and Wilde, 2003: 50). But, in Nordin's opinion, humanoids have no commercial potential – unlike special robots that can perform only special duties. Humanoids are good for studying AI.

But according to Nordin, even non-humanoid robots are often treated as humans. An elderly woman in Sweden, for example, apparently bought two grass clippers so the first one would not feel alone. Also, Nordin noticed, Facebook users were responding "R.I.P." to the demise of the Mars Exploration Rover.

In the future, robots will do all dirty, dull, and dangerous (DDD) jobs, and household duties. But Nordin believed that entertainment and company robots will be first; after all, "humanoid is the ultimate service robot" (Nordin and Wilde, 2003: 81). Humanoids will be especially useful in servicing other machines. What is more, "NASA believes in humanoids. In space research it is very important to have human-like robots." (p. 82). As to therapeutic robots such as Paro, the famous Japanese baby seal, Nordin thought it would be better if people cared about one another and left robots to produce cars, but he admitted that the younger generations may have different opinions on the matter.

A whole section of Nordin's book is dedicated to "Our working life and living standards." Will robots cause unemployment, or will people simply monitor them at work? History says that there may be problems at the beginning, including sabotage. (Apparently, "sabotage" comes from the *sabots* [wooden clogs] that French weavers used to demolish the new machines during the Industrial Revolution.) It is obviously valuable to ensure that criminals do not equip themselves with robots. And it is likely that there will be need for a universal basic income (a thought that has returned in most of the texts from the 2000s).

Nordin was the next writer after Margaret Atwood who observed that robots will be gobbling up a great deal of energy as their numbers increase, but he thought they may be using less energy than the current machines, or even learn to produce it themselves. In general, he declared his belief in "evolutionary robotics," which uses "genetic programming," and more specifically, the "thirty apes in a bus" algorithm. (Randomly chosen apes are permitted to drive the bus, and those that do the best job are allowed to reproduce.)

7.1.5 Sketches from Another Future

Andrew Pickering's 2010 book is actually a history of cybernetics in relation to psychology and psychiatry – not our focus at all. He does, however, make some interesting observations. He saw cybernetics as the opposite of modern rationality, as possibly "another future," partly in tune with James Scott's *Seeing like a state* and Bruno Latour's *We have never been modern* (which Pickering considered too conservative, however). One can wonder if people are really prepared to live in an anarchic, revealing mode (rather than enframing mode – Heidegger is constantly evoked).

Pickering had his own, highly positive interpretation of cybernetics, far from the governance:

> The modern sciences background their own practice, organizing it around a telos of knowledge production and then constructing it retrospectively in terms of that knowledge (a tale of errors dispelled). We [the readers] have seen that cybernetics was not like that. Cybernetics was about systems – human, nonhuman, or both – that staged their own performative dances of agency, that foregrounded performance rather than treating it as some forgettable background to knowledge. This is the primary sense in which one can read cybernetics as ontological theater – as forcibly reminding us of the domain of practice and performance and bringing it to the fore. As showing us, in a fascinating range of instances, that performance is not necessarily about knowledge, and that when knowledge comes into the picture it is as *part of* performance. (Pickering, 2010: 381)

In a note on page 474, Pickering explained his way of understanding "practice" and "performance" – words that

> … point in the same direction, though in different ways. "Practice" refers to human activity in the world, while "performance" is the "doing" of any entity or system, human or nonhuman. "Practice" is thus a subset of "performance."

We return to the notion of performance and theater in our discussion about Japanese robotics.

7.2   2010s: THE DECADE OF THE ROBOTS

In what follows, we omit two bestsellers: Kurzweil's *The singularity is near* (2005) and Boström's *Superintelligence* (2014), as they are not directly relevant to our topic. If a superintelligence takes over the world, loss of jobs will be the last thing on the (human) mind …

7.2.1   The Folly of Technological Solutions

Evgeny Morozov is best known as the author of a 2012 article entitled "A robot stole my Pulitzer!," to which we return in our discussion of the professions threatened by robotization. In his 2013 book, he severely criticized the "solutionists" – those people, most of whom are from Silicon Valley, who, to use garbage-can vocabulary (Cohen et al., 1972) are looking for problems to which they can apply their ready-made solutions.

> Silicon Valley's quest to fit us all into a digital straightjacket by promoting efficiency, transparency, certitude, and perfection—and, by extension, eliminating their evil twins of friction, opacity, ambiguity, and imperfection—will prove to be prohibitively expensive in the long run. (loc. 166)

Morozov quoted the distinction between *technoneutrals* and *technostructuralists*, introduced by Majid Tehranian, a US–Iranian political scientist. Technoneutrals believe (or at least claim) that technologies are neutral and can be used for either good or bad purposes. Technostructuralists relate the use of technologies to the existing power structures; their impact is always mediated by the current institutional order. This does not mean that technostructuralists are pessimists – merely that they consider each technology in the context of its most likely use.

> Yes, Google's self-driving cars would make driving easier and perhaps even cut the number of deaths on the road, but a reasonable transportation system ought to pursue many other objectives. Would self-driving cars result in inferior public transportation as more people took up driving? Would it lead to even greater suburban sprawl as, now that no longer had to drive, people could do e-mail during their commute and thus would tolerate spending more time in the car? (Morozov, 2013: 170–171)

Further on, he took up the issue discussed by Hayles: the error of assuming that humans are organic machines:

> None of this is to deny that technology (…) can be used to improve the human condition (…). But this can happen only if our geeks, designers, and social engineers take the time to study what makes us human in the first place. Trying to improve the human condition by first assuming that humans are like robots is not going to get us very far. (p. 350)

The final conclusion in the book is that "[t]echnology is not the enemy; our enemy is the romantic and revolutionary problem solver who resides within" (p. 358).

7.2.2   As Technology Races Ahead, It's Leaving Some People Behind

Brynjolfsson and McAfee's book *The second machine age* (2014) has become such a bestseller that a second edition was released in 2016. Indeed, we have quoted the book – and those who quoted the book – several times already in this book. Its conclusions, already presented in the introduction, are threefold: Digital technology has made astonishing progress recently, its results will be "profoundly beneficial," but they will be accompanied by some "thorny challenges." The authors quoted both Moravec's paradox, and its version as formulated by Steven Pinker: "The main lesson of thirty-five years of AI research is that the hard problems are easy and the easy problems are hard." (loc. 472). Although both they and Pinker are somewhat wrong in diagnosing what is hard and what is easy (throughout the book they don't believe that robots will be able to cook, for instance), the problem is well known, with many examples of simple actions performed by small children that are still impossible for robots. But the roboticists are working on it.

Brynjolfsson and McAfee have quoted Rodney Brooks, one of the roboticists trying to overcome Moravec's paradox. Brooks first founded iRobot, and then Rethink Robots, with a challenge aimed exactly at Morozov's criticisms: trying to teach robots to perform tasks that do not require precision. So, if this issue can be solved, what are the "thorny challenges" that remain?

> Advances in technology, especially digital technologies, are driving an unprecedented reallocation of wealth and income. Digital technologies can replicate valuable ideas, insights, and innovations at very low cost. This creates bounty for society and wealth for innovators, but diminishes the demand for previously important types of labor, which can leave many people with reduced incomes. The combination of bounty and spread challenges two common though contradictory worldviews. One common view is that advances in technology always boost incomes. The other is that automation hurts workers' wages as people are replaced by machines. Both of these have a kernel of truth, but the reality is more subtle. Rapid advances in our digital tools are creating unprecedented wealth, but there is no economic law that says all workers, or even a majority of workers, will benefit from these advances. (loc. 1910)

This observation contradicts the well-established conviction that wages increase with productivity and that automation threatens only manual jobs. Quoting research by their colleagues Acemoglu and Autor (2011),

Brynjolfsson and McAfee claimed that the important distinction is not cognitive vs. manual, but routine vs. non-routine jobs. So, the "techno-logical unemployment" predicted by Keynes in the 1930s (and quoted by almost every author of the works described in our text) may happen soon, if further development follows or even exceeds Moore's law.[3]

The solution? Brynjolfsson and McAfee still believe that "ideation, creativity and innovation" will remain human properties, but they suggest that "partnership between Dr. Watson and a human doctor will be far more creative and robust than either of them working alone" (loc. 2827): collaborative robots (and humans wishing to collaborate), plus the basic income.

7.2.3   Technology and the Threat Of Mass Unemployment

Martin Ford (2015) addressed many of the same issues as Brynjolfsson and McAfee did. For many years, especially after the World War II, there was a symbiosis between technological progress and the welfare of the workforce. No longer. Nowadays, "machines themselves are turning into workers, and the line between the capability of labor and capital is blurring as never before" (loc. 117). It is not exactly routine jobs that are threatened, though. (Ford preferred the adjective "predictable.") This threat and other changes could mean that "we may face the prospect of a 'perfect storm' where the impacts from soaring inequality, technological unemployment, and climate change unfold roughly in parallel, and in some ways amplify and reinforce each other" (loc. 211). Yes, the USA will "reshore" many of the jobs now offshored to China, but the number of the new jobs will be not in proportion to those that have been lost. The main disruption will occur in the service sector, where – at least in the

---

[3]   Gordon Moore, CEO of Intel, predicted in 1965 that the number of transis-tors in a dense integrated circuit will double every year, then changed it in 1975 to every second year. Now he believes they will be eliminated around 2025.

USA – most people are currently employed. According to Ford, three main forces will reshape the present retail sector:

> The first will be the continuing disruption of the industry by online retailers like Amazon, eBay, and Netflix. (...)
>
> The second transformative force is likely to be the explosive growth of the fully automated self-service retail sector—or, in other words, intelligent vending machines and kiosks. (...)
>
> The third major force likely to disrupt employment in the retail sector will be the introduction of increased automation and robotics into stores as high street retailers strive to remain competitive. (loc. 493–522)

Ford accepted the idea of collaboration, but was not as optimistic as Brynjolfsson and McAfee had been: "if you find yourself working with, or under the direction of, a smart software system, it's probably a pretty good bet that—whether you're aware of it or not—you are also training the software to ultimately replace you" (loc. 2140). He discussed the new areas in which the entrance of robots is relatively new, and we return to his insights in a later section in this chapter. In general, he warned against the exaggerated optimism of technology fans:

> The threat to overall employment is that as creative destruction unfolds, the "destruction" will fall primarily on labor-intensive businesses in traditional areas like retail and food preparation, while the "creation" will generate new businesses and industries that simply don't hire many people. In other words, the economy is likely on a path toward a tipping point where job creation will begin to fall consistently short of what is required to fully employ the workforce. (loc. 2812)

Comparing the present "rise of the robots" with previous technological revolution, Ford noticed that in 1964 the so-called Ad Hoc Committee on the Triple Revolution, which included chemist Linus Pauling and economist Gunnar Myrdal, had proposed the implementation of a guaranteed minimum income, made possible by the economy of abundance created by progressing automation. At present, "some form of direct redistribution of purchasing power becomes essential if economic growth is to continue" (loc. 4292). As to the energy problems, solar power is certainly a promising solution, but not without its own complications – the costs of equipment, installation and maintenance of solar panels, for example.

7.2.4 Is It Different This Time?

This question has been asked by practically every author we have quoted, and Nigel M. de S. Cameron (2017) basically reviewed various answers to the question (including writers who criticized Ford for his pessimism). Cameron arrived at the following conclusions:

> The prospect of a major disruption involving large-scale structural unemployment might be unlikely–but only if one (or both) of two assumptions can be made.
>
> First, if the future is one in which the impact of Machine Intelligence on existing employment is significantly less than many have predicted. This could be for various reasons. Perhaps the predictions are simply wrong and the Oxford and Pew studies should simply be discounted. Perhaps the technology will take much longer to be applied. Or perhaps we humans will just prove more resistant to the handover than predicted. (…)
>
> A second justification for discounting our concerns, perhaps more realistic than the first (…), would in fact require three separate components in the scenario for it to work. First, the rapid arrival of new jobs. Second, it involves the assumption that the new jobs will come in diverse and large quantities. Third, the education and training programs required to convert workers in the current economy into candidates for these diverse new opportunities need to be effective and timely. This may be the greatest stretch of all. (loc. 1127–1158)

He also mentioned a Universal Basic Income (UBI), claiming that it was Milton Friedman who first suggested it.[4] Under discussion for great many years, it is a policy proposal that "takes on a fresh life."

7.2.5 Hearts Instead of Hands and Heads?

The most recent book by Richard Baldwin (2019) combines global robotization and "telemigrants" – people who work via telecommunication for a company situated in another country. Like the authors before him, he reviewed the history of technology (in fact, his book could have been entitled *The third machine age*), concluding that the "digitech" is radically different from both the steam and the ICT. The difference lies in the fact that machines can learn now, and intelligence is not only artificial (AI), but also remote (RI) – thanks to the teleworkers. Yet "[m]achines have not been very successful at acquiring social intelligence, emo-

---

[4] Most likely it was Thomas Paine who coined the concept of the "guaranteed minimum income" in 1797 (Haagh, 2019).

tional intelligence, creativity, innovativeness, or the ability to deal with unknown situations" (loc. 206).

According to Baldwin, robots will eliminate many jobs but few occupations. Here is the list of industries in which jobs will vanish:

- retail
- construction
- security
- food preparation
- transportation
- medical care
- pharmacies
- journalism
- legal work
- finance.

No wonder Andrew Yang, a Democrat candidate for US president, protested the ongoing automation.

> If we don't change things dramatically, children will grow up in a country with fewer and fewer opportunities and a handful of companies and individuals reaping the gains from the new technologies while the rest of us struggle to find opportunities and lose our jobs. (loc. 161)

Andrew Yang is not the only one to be concerned: Baldwin quoted Bill Gates, Elon Musk, Jeff Bezos and Stephen Hawking among those who held similar beliefs. In the end, this is Yang's solution:

> Three rules will help prepare ourselves and our children for the globotics revolution. These are just common sense. First, seek jobs that don't compete directly with white-collar robots (AI) or telemigrants (RI). Second, seek to build up skills that allow you to avoid direct competition with RI and with AI. Third, realize that humanity is an edge not a handicap. (…)
> In the future, having a good heart may be as important to economic success as having a good head was in the twentieth century, and a strong hand was in the nineteenth century. (loc. 4200–4203)

This view, which has to be called romantic, is based on the assumption that

> [t]he sheltered sectors of the future will be those where people actually have to be together doing things for which humanity is an edge. This will mean that our work lives will be filled with far more caring, sharing, understanding,

creating, empathizing, innovating, and managing people who are actually in the same room. (loc. 212)

Let us hope he is right. In the meantime though, the avatar Amelia, that has been referred to by Baldwin as a successful "thinking computer," has been "fired" from one bank that used it,[5] because she brought no cost reduction. And although Amelia is supposed to be working for the bank that one of us has been using since 2016, there is no trace of it on the website anymore. Not empathetic enough?

In the section that follows, we refer to social science texts focusing on society sectors into which robotization has only recently entered.

7.3   ROBOTS ARE HERE!

Although there is considerable use of robots in military and security contexts, this is not a new phenomenon; on the other hand, robots in construction work are so new that we prefer not to express any decisive opinions. We have chosen those areas that were mentioned by the largest number of authors we read.

7.3.1   Self-driving Cars

We have already quoted Morozov's (2013) divided opinion on the usefulness of self-driving cars, and indeed, most opinions are divided, although the existence and use of such cars seems to be generally taken for granted. Furthermore, information about them is divided: Will truck drivers be the first (Cameron, 2017; Baldwin, 2019) or the last (Ford, 2015) to lose their jobs? Some commentators suggest that enthusiasm is premature. Ford (2015) claimed that the first self-driving cars weren't able to perform even 10 percent of their tasks (loc. 2905); yet the general public believes that everybody can make a call from their smartphone, and a self-driving car will be delivered. And if the motor industry is truly geared toward automation, it may be because of legal problems that automation is still only partial:

> Chris Urmson, one of the engineers who led Google's car project, said at an industry conference in 2013 that concerns over ambiguity are misplaced,

---

[5]   https://www.finextra.com/newsarticle/32371/nordnet-fires-ai-assistant -amelia, accessed May 7, 2019.

and that current US law makes it clear that the car's manufacturer would be responsible in the event of an accident. It's hard to imagine anything the motor industry would fear more. (Ford, 2015: loc. 2936)

That was in 2013, however. Two years later, "Volvo has taken the lead in stating that it will accept full liability – a policy that may set the standard for other manufacturers" (Cameron, 2017, loc. 506).

Cameron also reminded the readers of the doubtful achievements in the first attempts at self-driving cars in Detroit, but had more faith in roboticists. In general, he was in favor of self-driving cars with no human control:

> It may seem counter-intuitive, but a major argument in favor of self-driving technology is safety. While we find the notion of 70 mph freeway traffic without a driver's hands on the wheel a scary prospect, the fact is that we humans are not really very good at many of the things we do ... (loc.493)
>
> Moreover, the prospect is not simply that vehicles will drive more safely than humans currently do, but that they will also drive defensively. With 360-degree awareness at all times, and communication with other vehicles (around corners, for example), they should protect passengers from the mistakes of other drivers as well. (loc. 501)

Why total automation? "Keeping half-focused on the driving process – for human drivers who tend not to focus properly even when they are supposed to be driving entirely on their own – seems particularly dangerous" (loc. 519).

Yet, as quoted by Baldwin (2019), US Democrat candidate Andrew Yang was against it: "All you need is self-driving cars to destabilize society (...) That one innovation will be enough to create riots in the street" (loc. 161).

7.3.2   Journalism

Evgeny Morozov's "A robot stole my Pulitzer!" article (2012) has been widely read, probably because he was discussing the dangers of automated journalism and automated trading, which we explore in the next section. His main target was the website and the company, known as Narrative Science:

> Narrative Science is one of several companies developing automated journalism software. These startups work primarily in niche fields—sports, finance, real estate—in which news stories tend to follow the same pattern and revolve

around statistics. Now they are entering the political reporting arena, too. A new service from Narrative Service generates articles about how the U.S. electoral race is reflected in social media, what issues and candidates are most and least discussed in a particular state or region, and similar topics. It can even incorporate quotes from the most popular and interesting tweets into the final article. Nothing covers Twitter better than the robots. (p. 3)

Why are Narrative Science algorithms better than live journalists? They are cheaper and quicker, they never get sick, and they never get upset. Morozov admitted all that, along with the fact that the mechanical duties of Narrative Science may free the (remaining) journalists to spend more time on more ambitious projects. His main concern, however, had to do with the accessibility of reading habits that the use of Narrative Science permits, which opens the possibility of keeping the readers in self-reproducing circles of information, thereby introducing the chance of "hurting the civil discourse," as mentioned in the subtitle of his article.

One of us (Czarniawska, 2013) observed the automation of news production in news agencies. Did it liberate the creative potential of humans, as Narrative Science promised? That did not seem to be the case. Rather, increased automation meant more and more new duties for humans, along with a requirement for their greater and greater speed. If they had time to do so, news producers could probably have greater influence over programmers, or they could extend the use of the programs in new and innovative ways. In contrast to young hackers, who can spend days and nights tinkering with software, the news producers are adult family members with normal lives, and their working time is structured primarily by the demand of speed. "I wish we had more time to reflect," sighed a journalist at the Swedish agency TT during an interview (Czarniawska, 2013: 9). But the speed required of her was still slow compared to that at which so-called robo-trading, or algorithmic trading happens.

7.3.3   Accounting and Finance

The past decade has witnessed the emergence of algorithmic trading models designed to read data and trade automatically. In electronic financial markets, algorithmic trading or automated trading is also known as algo-trading or robo-trading. It consists of using computer programs for entering trading orders with the help of a computer algorithm. It is used primarily by managers of hedge funds, pension funds, mutual funds, and other institutional investments. There is a special software called Real

Time Economic Data for feeding algo-traders' terminals, and a polling unit (STEEL POLL) that is constantly polling financial strategies and determining the formal consensus reached on forecasts. The average forecast is plugged into Real Time Economic Data; the trading computers pick it up and execute the trade. For example, USA releases an unemployment report, first showing what the forecasters foresaw and then showing that the actual situation is worse. The US dollar decreases in value and bonds increase, and as the traders compete in speed, the computers beat the humans. The problem is that there could be an initial violent price move, but then a qualification follows: the unemployment data differed in different seasons. After 30 seconds or so, the human beings come in again, as the journalists offer their interpretation (Czarniawska, 2013). But algo-trading has its downside:

5 October 2010
WASHINGTON (Reuters)—U.S. regulators are investigating trading algorithms after they found that a computer-driven sale helped trigger May's flash crash, Securities and Exchange Commission Chairman Mary Schapiro said on Tuesday. (…) An SEC and Commodity Futures Trading Commission report found that the single trade, worth $4.1 billion, by a single trader helped trigger the brief crash May 6. The Dow Jones industrial average plunged 700 points in minutes before recovering. The SEC was already grappling with changes in the equity markets before the flash crash. Now the regulator is under political and public pressure to fix the fragmented markets, dominated by lightning computer trading on dozens of mostly electronic exchanges and alternative venues. Regulations have not kept up with markets, Schapiro said.

Economists defend algo-trading, claiming that it contributes to more efficient pricing and that it has had a small but positive impact on market liquidities. No signs of increased volatility were discovered by Chaboud et al. (2014), for example. They did mention the flash crash in one sentence of their paper, but it did not change their conclusions, and the regulators did nothing, either.

Lawyers are not particularly optimistic, however – not only about algo-trading, but also about automated banking and finance. Here is a fragment of an abstract from an article by a lawyer from Temple University:

A sea change is happening in finance. Machines appear to be on the rise and humans on the decline. Human endeavors have become unmanned endeavors. Human thought and human deliberation have been replaced by computerized analysis and mathematical models. Technological advances have made finance faster, larger, more global, more interconnected, and less human. Modern finance is becoming an industry in which the main players are no longer entirely human. Instead, the key players are now cyborgs: part machine, part human. Modern finance is transforming into what this article calls cyborg finance. (Lin, 2013: 680)

"The end is near for human investor," is the opening sentence of Lin's article. But the end is not totally pessimistic:

The choice of humans versus machines is a false one because every human is a cyborg now. We are all part human and part machine. The competition of the future is not a competition of humans *against* machines but a competition among humans *with* machines. The future of cyborg finance is not about what machines can do to humans but about what humans can do with machines. (ss. 733–734)

Collaborative robots, then, and sensible regulators. How about lawyers?

7.3.4   Legal Work

According to Ford (2015), the lawyers and paralegals who spent time sorting out paper documents will be replaced by robots. Law firms will then need lawyers who are able to collaborate with robots or do anything they are told to do, as there are apparently too many law graduates in USA and UK. But even if these young lawyers will accept practically any job at any price, the robots will still be cheaper. As to the collaboration, "while human-machine collaboration jobs will certainly exist, they seem likely to be relatively few in number and often short-lived. In a great many cases, they may also be un-rewarding or even dehumanizing." (loc. 2173)

Some law firms have found the solution by specializing in the employment issues typical for robotics (Cameron, 2017). Baldwin (2019), optimistic as usual, believes that artificial intelligence could create many jobs for engineers, accountants, tax specialists, and investment advisors, and for people to teach others to perform the basic tasks of lawyers. This development will not threaten professional jobs, he argued, because it will make many professional services more affordable and thus create a whole new demand for these new services.

7.3.5   Healthcare and Care for the Elderly

The major discussion of robotization concerns healthcare and care for
the elderly. The reasons are many. To begin with, many countries face
an aging population that lives longer and longer, requiring more care,
and the choice is sometimes between robots and immigrants. More and
more sophisticated machines (not necessarily robots as such) are being
used in medicine. In this section we compare a Swedish field study of the
encounters between robots and the elderly with the Japanese approach to
robots in care.

Susanne Frennert (2016) observed elderly people in their experimental domestic use of the three types of robots: GiraffPlus (an e-Health
monitoring robot), HOBBIT (an assistive robot), and a vacuum cleaner.
She concluded that the designers followed a technological deterministic
approach, assuming that they knew everything there was to know about
the users and believing that robots can be constructed and tested according to "fixed criteria and quantitative measurements at baseline, midway
and post-intervention" (p. 95). This assumption includes a perception
of elderly people as weak, ill, and homebound. This impression is in
accordance with an earlier study (Gustavsson and Czarniawska, 2004),
which demonstrated that the construction of a "web woman" (an avatar)
was based on a stereotypical image of the ideal worker, even though the
goal of the designers – all women – was to abolish stereotypes.

Strangely enough, the elderly persons who were asked to use the
robots were completely in agreement with that stereotypical picture of
the elderly, although it was not consistent with their self-image. In their
opinion, robots will be truly helpful to other people – who were much
older and seriously weak, ill, and homebound.

Another observation to which Frennert paid little attention was
a common pattern of sensemaking (which she called "meaning making,"
obviously having never heard of Weick, 1995) that interpreted robots as
"servants":

> I got a female servant!
> Her name is Dusty – but don't think it's strange. She is a robot. Her specialty
> is dust. She's not very intelligent and that's why her full name is Dust Dummy.
> After a tour in the living room, hallway and kitchen she stops and blinks. She
> is full with compact load of dust bunnies. I thought the place was clean but

she reveals my secrets – that rascal! She hesitates when confronted with paper scraps and sand, and straight out rejects paper clips and small nails.

She's a pleasant acquaintance – I let her out from time to time. She parks at a docking station in the living room and is easiest to operate by remote control. One click and she wakes up, one more and she is at my service with a nice humming sound. I worry about what she does in the hallway. She moves my shoes and I think that's where she gets tipsy. (p. 12)

This was a letter written to the researcher by one of the participants who never read the dissertation, as he died before it was finished. But to avoid the suspicion that this patronizing attitude is typical only of men, here is a fragment from an interview with a woman:

I would much rather have a robot than human help because the robot does what I tell it to do, while what the homecare staff does is based on a list of what to do and when. If I have robot help then I will not have to instruct a new person each time. A robot does not gossip and I do not like to have strangers in my home. I trust the robot and robot does not steal. You cannot control another person as I can control the robot. Many fear that a robot will replace human contact, but a robot does not exclude human contact, instead the robot will be my servant. (p. 103)

Frennert observed that robots nourish the desire for freedom, control, and independence (of course in relation to those much older persons who will be the final users – or even themselves at a much older age).

Frennert's final conclusion, which is truly to be applauded, is that the designers should adopt a practice-oriented approach, in the sense of actually trying out their prototypes rather than asking opinions about them, as another of her observations was that "there is a difference between what older people say and what they do."[6]

She tried also to explain why Swedes in particular and Europeans in general, in contrast to the Japanese, are against the idea of robots taking care of elderly people. (She quoted a Swedish study from 1998 and a Eurobarometer from 2012, p. 45). Respondents who answered the survey were positive about robots doing DDD jobs – but not about taking care of people.

Sone's (2017) main argument in his book on Japanese robots is that "the widely discussed Japanese affinity for the robots" is correct, but it is too narrowly explained by some essentialist and static image of

---

[6] This could be said of respondents of all ages.

"the Japanese culture." Instead, it is, "the outcome of a complex loop of representation and expectation that is also an ideological iteration within Japan's continuing struggle with modernity" (p. 1).

Japan has been automating its industry sector since the late 1960s, which has contributed to the country's famous economic success. And both robotization and economic success continued throughout the 1980s. In the new millennium, a new problem emerged: a labor shortage due to the country's rapidly aging population. The government reacted by sponsoring research and construction of new robot prototypes, designed to work in hospitals, offices, and homes. This development continues.

So, yes, it makes sense to contrast Japanese and Western attitudes toward robots, but only on the assumption that this contrast has been changing with the times and that it was actually an interaction. Sone chose "a performance studies approach," because "the popular view of the robot in Japan is expressed in terms of the operation of theatre." In fact, most of the cases he analyzed concerned the dramatic presentations of robots.

The advanced Western countries also develop service and care robots, but in Japan these are anthropomorphic and zoomorphic figures. The anthropomorphic figures come in two variations: humanoids (metallic surfaces and roughly human bodies) and androids (skin-like surfaces and facial features).

Sone compared the definitions of robots as found in the *Oxford English Dictionary*, the *ISO 9001 Quality Manual*, the Japanese Industrial Standards, and a report entitled "Japan's Robot Strategy" commissioned by Japan's Ministry of Economy, Trade and Industry. In all four contexts there is a distinction between industrial robots and the newly introduced non-industrial robots, called usually service robots.

> There is a subtle difference between the OED and Japanese dictionaries ... While the meaning of the robot as automated machine is similar, the Japanese dictionaries describe a robot as automaton or artificial person and as a person who is controlled like a puppet. (...) The OED stresses that robot is a machine. Taken together, the two definitions in the Japanese dictionary indicate the robot as a both an artificial person and as a person who is controllable. (p. 6)

This trait of controllability is criticized from the ethical point of view by such scholars as Turkle, but we return to that issue later. Sone's argument is that many Japanese people find the concept of an artificial human intriguing rather than frightening, because they do not have the associations that Westerners have with Frankenstein's monster and Golems.

Furthermore, Western robots are made "from dumb matter" (p. 9), whereas Japanese robots are grandchildren of nature, because humans are children of nature. It is Buddhism, the Japanese tradition of manga/anime, and animism (spirit incarnated in nature and in inanimate objects) that contribute to a positive perception of humanoid robots.[7]

But what about the "uncanny valley" – the concept launched by a Japanese roboticist? Yet, as described by Jasia Reichardt (1978), Mori predicted that as machines appear more and more human-like,

> people's sense and connection with them increases until at a certain point there is a sudden drop, a "valley" when robots become creepy (...). But, as robots increasingly resemble humans, the positive feeling towards them then increases, and at the highest level of resemblance, the perceiver's connection with the robot is like an affinity for a healthy human. (Sone, 2017: 17)

As to service robots, the Humanoid Robotics Project (1998–2003), financed by the Japanese government, asked roboticists to develop robots that could contribute to the management of an aging population: care robots, pet robots, nurse assistant robots, and even dementia-prevention robots.

> The engagement of dementia patients with therapeutic robots is seen positively by the proponents of those machines. Critics, on the other hand, look at the use of the social robot in aged care in terms of duplicity and control. (p. 191)

Sherry Turkle provided the primary example of such a critique; she wishes to protect children and the elderly from such "deceptive" communication. In his defense, Sone described the uses of AIST's Paro the baby seal and Sony's Aibo the robot dog. (For reasons never mentioned in the book, Sony stopped Aibo's production in 2006, and the repair services

---

[7]   The fact that AI is used in astrology in India suggests that attitudes towards digitalization in general, and robotization in particular, may differ strongly across cultures. (See https://www.astrocamp.com/bhrigoo-ai-powered-app-for-astrology.html, accessed June 11, 2019.)

ceased in 2014.[8]) Both have been used as "socially assistive robots" in USA, Australia, and Japan.

> Assistive robot refers to a robotic machine that "assists people with physical disabilities through physical interaction" for domestic and institutional use (…). The term "socially assistive robot" delineates a subcategory within assistive robots, which refers to robots that provide a assistance to humans, through interaction with verbal and/or physical gesture but without physical contact (…). Socially assistive robots have been used as companions or guides for the elderly and children … (p. 193)

Many hopes are connected to socially assistive robots, but some problems remain unsolved: the high cost and technical complexity of implementation, together with lack of agreement on ways of measuring their effectiveness. In Sone's opinion, it is time for social scientists and humanists to join the roboticists in their work. At present, "[t]he wide-spread justification (…) for the use of socially assistive robots in aged care is often based on a commonly held view that the Japanese prefer robots over human helpers, especially foreign health workers" (p. 194)

Western social scientists have analyzed the Japanese use of robots and concluded that it means

> a decrease in human contact, the mistreatment of elderly patients as objects, and the loss of control over one's own life (…) There is a strong view that the idea of robot companion and its presumed benefits are "premised on people believing that robots are something that they are not." (Sone, 2017: 195)

Sone argued that robots make better pets than animals do because animals carry germs, can bite and scratch, and eventually die, causing sorrow. He described the use of the dog Aibo for therapy, and concluded that

> [t]he use of robots for therapy involves a kind of theatrical structure: with the facilitator as MC [Master of Ceremonies], robots as performers, and patients as the audience. (…) the elderly person knows that robots are not alive, yet they are able to treat them as if they are living creatures. (p. 197)

Paro the seal is supposed to reduce people's expectations. (Most people know what to expect from cats and dogs and can be disappointed, but they don't know what to expect from a baby seal.) "Paro embodies

---

[8]   But see http://mentalfloss.com/article/505183/aibo-sony's-failed-robot -dog-returning-smart-home-device, accessed April 28, 2019.

cuddliness and cuteness" (p. 202). But ethical problems remain: Those enchanted with the dog Aibo (mostly children) could make their own decision about buying the machine; Paro was "forced upon" the elderly.[9]

Sone's conclusions:

> Aiming to address the caregiving needs of rapidly ageing Japanese population, the use of socially assistive robots for aged care is in fact an experiment that is based on the idea of "technological fix", as part of Japan's greater reliance on technology for twenty-first-century solutions to its economic and social problems.
>
> [Japanese] traditions promote the idea that humans and non-humans are viewed intrinsically as connected. The robot's radical difference is perceived through what might be termed a functional anthropomorphism; at the same time, by seeing them in such a way, human interactants can develop a certain affection for the non-human and, in this case, for robots. (pp. 204–207)

Perhaps such a possibility is open even to people who do not share the traditions of Buddhism and animism.

---

[9]   Fiona Moore (2016) made Paro the main character in a horror story ...

8.   (Some) conclusions

As many of the sources we quoted and analyzed repeat the same or similar messages, we shall keep our conclusions short and refer only to the main topics mentioned in all types of literature.

As to Singularity, humans will likely cross that bridge when they come to it. For the time being, this topic of discussion fits mostly the debates between the roboticists and the philosophers, while remaining an attractive theme for science fiction writers and movie producers. One comment that struck us as insightful and especially well informed has been offered by a UK neurosurgeon, Henry Marsh, in his article "Can man ever build a mind?" (2019).

There are and there will be many uses for robots in the military context; there are many legal and ethical issues to consider,[1] but most of them will not be related to work and jobs.

Industries will continue to be automated, with a great deal of attention paid to collaborative robots (cobots).[2] Yet some critical scholars, like Peter Fleming, who launched the concept of "bounded automation" (2018), claim that the more easily threatened and underpaid jobs may actually proliferate before robotization, because "it is not technology that determines employment patterns or organizational design but the other way around" (p. 28).

Self-driving cars are apparently just around the corner; yet few people will give up driving – simply because many people like it. The self-driving cars may open new possibilities for persons with physical disabilities; whether or not they will threaten the jobs of professional drivers remains to be seen.[3]

As to health and elder care, it may differ among countries. Although the Japanese apparently have nothing against being cared for by robots,

---

[1]   See e.g. Liljefors, Noll and Steuer, 2019.

[2]   *The Collaborative Robot Buyer's Guide* already exists. https://www .engineering.com/ResourceMain.aspx?resid=486, accessed June 3, 2019.

[3]   In her science fiction detective novel, *Driving Ambitions* (2018), Fiona Moore assumes that self-driving taxis will even form the unions...

our interviews concerning the future of welfare in Sweden (Czarniawska and Solli, 2019) revealed another situation considered ideal. The ill and the elderly should be provided with a steady human contact (a physician or a nurse), plus an intelligent machine or machines that can do all possible tests and analyze them – the same with specialized and emergency situations. In short: AI, yes. Robots, no.

Among the white-collar professionals who seemed to be most threatened by robotization are journalists, lawyers, and accountants. Whether they will vanish or merely diminish, as the mechanical part of such jobs are removed, only the future will show. (We do not want to risk repeating Jasia Reinhardt's error by predicting the future.)

What we dare to do is to predict some developments within the debate on robotization and its consequences. The debate may change the ways in which various jobs are described and categorized: Which, exactly, are the dull, dirty, and dangerous jobs? Which jobs are routine and predictable, and which are not? Take as an example a security job: Nothing may happen for hours, days, or even months, and then the most unforeseeable can occur.

The work of roboticists in different countries and users' reactions to them suggest that reactions to robots may vary among cultures, the global economy notwithstanding. No matter which culture, though, the literature we reviewed strongly signals that robot designers should be collaborating with psychologists and social scientists before – not after – they commence their design work. Their collaboration may partly even out the loss of jobs as, obviously, all professions related to IT, AI, and robotization will expand.

The issues that remain unsolved are costs, energy sources, and income. Among the solutions most often proposed are solar energy, basic income, and a tax on robots.

The Metropolitan Policy Program at Brookings (Muro, Maxim and Whiton, 2019), also using the 2017 report from the McKinsey Global Institute, ended with the conclusion that almost no occupation will be unaffected by the adoption of currently available technologies. Still, as predicted, the routine physical and cognitive tasks will be the most vulnerable to automation in the coming years. After having analyzed it, their commentary on the literature is quite in accordance with our beliefs as well:

> The power and prospect of automation and artificial intelligence (AI) initially alarmed technology experts, for fear that machine advancements would

destroy jobs. Then came a correction of sorts, with a wave of reassurances minimizing their negative impacts.

Now, the discourse appears to be arriving at a more complicated, mixed understanding that suggests that automation will bring neither apocalypse nor utopia, but instead both benefits and stresses alike. Such is the ambiguous and sometimes disembodied nature of the "future of work" discussion. (p. 4)

Appendix: Sources used in media analysis (Chapter 6)[1]

2014

1. Kelly, Gavin, "The robots are coming. Will they bring wealth or divided society?," *The Guardian*, January 4.
2. Boeing, Nils "New jobs for robots," *Die Zeit*, February 28.
3. https://www.thedailybeast.com/relax-robots-wont-take-every-job-the-second-machine-age, accessed March 14, 2014.
4. Belfiore, Michael, "When robots take our jobs, humans will be the new 1%. Here's how to fight back," *The Guardian*, March 22.
5. https://robotenomics.com/2014/04/16/study-indicates-robots-could-replace-80-of-jobs/, April 16, accessed January 9, 2020.
6. http://blogs.faz.net/10vor8/2014/05/16/gesetzlose-gesellen-wenn-roboter-knoellchen-bekommen-1426/, May 16 , accessed January 9, 2020.
7. http://www.huffingtonpost.com/stephen-hawking/artificial-intelligence_b_5174265.html, accessed July 7, 2016.
8. Lundgren, Eva, "I väntan på de intelligenta robotarna," *GU Journalen*, June, 14–15.
9. Myers, Joshua, "Robo-Morality: Can philosophers program ethical codes into robots?," *Humanist*, July/August.
10. https://www.forbes.com/sites/ryancalo/2014/07/17/could-cynthia-breazeal-prove-the-steve-wozniak-of-robots/#2e570f015e93, accessed January 9, 2020.
11. Hern, Alex, "Wikipedia: meet the man who has edited 3m articles," *The Guardian*, August 5.

---

[1] Observe how at certain points in time, the media in a given country concentrate on the same topic, like the Swedish media in April 2015. No authors are quoted when the text is a piece of news or an interview.

12. Piesing, Mark, "Medical robotics: Would you trust a robot with a scalpel?," *The Observer*, October 10

13. http://www.roboterwelt.de/magazin/studie-world-robotics-2014/, accessed October 13, 2014.

14. Davis, Nicola, "Dolls, pets, drones: six ways that robots will change the way we live," *The Observer*, October 19.

15. Gibbs, Samuel, "Elon Musk: artificial intelligence is our biggest existential threat," *The Guardian*, October 27.

16. Halpern, Sue, "The creepy new way of the internet," *New York Review of Books*, November 20.

17. https://www.bbc.com/news/technology-30290540, accessed December 2, 2014.

18. Atwood, Margaret, "Are humans necessary?," *New York Times*, December 4.

19. Aeppel, Timothy, "This wasn't written by an algorithm, but more and more is," *The Wall Street Journal*, December 15.

2015

20. https://www-welt-de/vermischtes/article 136018408/Wie-unse r-Leben-in-10-Jahren-aussehen-wird.html, January 5.

21. "Sono in arrivo i robot da compagnia," *La Stampa*, January 20.

22. Leslie, Ian, "Reign of the robots: how to live in the machine age," *New Statesman*, January 21.

23. "Dlaczego niektóre roboty wpadają w dolinę niesamowitości?," *Kulturoteka*, January 26.

24. Sparshott, Jeffrey, "The robots are coming for your paycheck," *The Wall Street Journal*, February 17.

25. https://www.svd.se/robot-i-aldrevard-etisk-utmaning, February 18, accessed January 9, 2020.

26. Lindgren, Håkan, "Tekniken är inte en naturkraft," *Svenska Dagbladet*, February 21.

27. Aeppel, Timothy, "Be calm, robots aren't about to take your job, MIT economist says," *The Wall Street Journal*, February 25.

28. Winter, Simon, "Datorer tar hälften av jobben inom 20 år," *Svenska Dagbladet*, April 3.

29. Bursell Jacob/Thomas Peterffy, "Skapade världens första automatiska börsrobot," *Svenska Dagbladet*, April 3.

30. https://www.edge.org/conversation/yuval_noah_harari-daniel _kahneman-death-is-optional, April 3, accessed January 9, 2020.

31. "Robotar tar över mer av vårt arbete," *Svenska Dagbladet*, April 5.
32. Sigander, Miranda, "Redo för robotar?," *GöteborgsPosten*, April 7.
33. Hagber, Mattias, "Drönaren kan aldrig känna sig skyldig," *GöteborgsPosten*, April 9.
34. "Automatisering en utmaning om fler jobb ska räddas," *Dagens Nyheter*, April 17.
35. Heickerö, Roland, "Automatisering skapar nya faror," *Svenska Dagbladet*, April 24.
36. "Robotarna tar över journalistiken," *Dagens Nyheter*, April 25.
37. "Dopo lo chef-robot, un algoritmo inventerà le ricette," *La Stampa*, April 27.
38. https://www.dn.se/kultur-noje/jakten-pa-kronikekoden/, May 10, accessed January 9, 2020.
39. "Walkman: ecco il robot umanoide italiano che usa il trapano e guida," *La Stampa*, May 13.
40. Irenius, Lisa, "Robotar är inte journalistikens fiender," *Svenska Dagbladet*, May 15.
41. Di Todaro, Fabio, "Alle Olimpidi dei robot Corea batte Italia," *La Stampa*, June 8.
42. Arthur, Charles, "Artificial intelligence: don't fear AI. It's already on your phone – and useful," *The Guardian*, June 15.
43. Baurmann, Jana Gioia, "Willkommen, Kollege!," *Die Zeit*, June 25.
44. Massing, Michael, "Digital journalism: The next generation," *The New York Review of Books*, June 25.
45. Adams, Tim, "And the Pulitzer goes to... a computer," *The Guardian*, June 28.
46. "I, researcher. How a professor's work with robots brings hope to older people," *Challenge Cardiff*, Summer 2015, June 29.
47. https://www.dn.se/ekonomi/robotarna-tar-plats-i-varden/, July 2, accessed January 9, 2020.
48. Deng, Boer, "The robot's dilemma," *Nature*, vol. 523, July 2.
49. Hooton, Christopher, "A robot has passed a self-awareness test," *The Independent*, July 17.
50. http://www.bbc.com/future/story/20150717-the-people-possessed -by-computers, accessed January 9, 2020.
51. "Robot zabójca nie czuje nienawiści," *Gazeta Wyborcza*, July 31.
52. https://cio.idg.se/2.1782/1.622535/filosofen--ai-ar-det-storsta -hotet-mot-manskligheten, August 7, accessed January 9, 2020.

53. https://blogs.faz.net/fazit/2015/08/14/was-wenn-roboter-uns-das -denken-adnehmen-6324/, August 14, accessed January 9, 2020.
54. "Automation angst," *The Economist*, August 15.
55. "Ecco Walk-man, il primo robot che sorregge in foto la Torre di Pisa," *La Stampa*, September 25.
56. Goldberg, Ken, "Countering singularity sensationalism," *Nature*, vol. 526, October 15.
57. "Är du redo att öppna ditt hem för en robot?," *Svenska Dagbladet*, an advertisement from European Media Partner, October 16.
58. https://qz.com/538260/human-values-should-be-programmed-into -robots-argues-a-computer-scientist/, October 31, accessed January 9, 2020.
59. "Digitalisera eller dö," *Affärslivet Industri*, November.
60. "Artificial intelligence: 'Homo sapiens will be split into a handful of gods and the rest of us,'" *The Guardian*, November 7.
61. Hern, Alex and Milmo, Dan, "Thinking machines: the skilled jobs that could be taken over by robots," *The Guardian*, November 12.
62. "Roboten tar över allt mer," *Göteborgs Posten*, November 22.
63. Gulliksen, Jan, "När roboterna gör det mesta av jobbet," *Göteborgs Posten*, November 25.
64. Szoldra, Paul, "8 industries robots will completely transform by 2025," *Business Insider*, December 2.
65. Wiseman, Eva, "Sex, love and robots: is this the end of intimacy?," *The Guardian*, December 13.
66. "Due italiane tra le star della robotica," *La Stampa*, December 22.

2016

67. "Hon vill lära roboten ta mänskliga beslut," *IVA Aktuellt*, January.
68. "Forskningsmiljarder till digitalisering av industrin," *IVA Aktuellt*, January.
69. "De tekniska utmaningarna är många," *IVA Aktuellt*, January.
70. Knoll, Andrew H., "Capturing Mars," *Science*, January 1.
71. https://www.welt.de/kultur/article151109141/Das-Jahr-der -Roboter-Wir-sind-dann-mal-weg.html, January 17, accessed January 9, 2020.
72. https://blogs.faz.net/fazit/2016/01/21/die-gewinner-der-vierten -industriellen-revolution-7254/, January 21, accessed January 9, 2020.

73. "Would you bet against sex robots? AI 'could leave half of world unemployed,'" *The Guardian*, February 13.
74. Cars, Göran, "Så kan vi bygga den framtida goda staden," *IVA Aktuellt*, February 18.
75. Musser, George, "Consciousness creep," *Scientific American*, February 25.
76. "Teknik ger glädje som spinn-off effekt," *Göteborgs Posten*, March 13.
77. Gelertner, David, "Machines that will think and feel," *The Wall Street Journal*, March 18.
78. Karén, Fredric, "Se upp – nu kommer robotarna," *Svenska Dagbladet*, March 20.
79. "När artificiell intelligens möter mänsklig dumhet," *Svenska Dagbladet*, April 2.
80. Winfield, Alan, "Should robots be gendered?," *Robohub*, April 20.
81. "Robothandlarna har tagit över Wall Street," *Svenska Dagbladet*, April 22.
82. Wortham, Rob, "How to design trustworthy robot butlers that we won't want to treat like humans," *The Conversation*, May 13.
83. Handman, Wren, "You can't talk about robots without talking about basic income," *Motherboard*, May 14.
84. "Forskningen rustar sig för artificiell intelligens," *Svenska Dagbladet*, May 15.
85. Bergström, Andreas and Roine, Jesper, "Automatisering har inte lett till utslagning av arbetskraft," *Dagens Nyheter*, May 22.
86. Wilks, Harvey, "I let a robot take over my social media for 48 hours," *Motherboard*, May 30.
87. Bland, Ben, "Industrial robots: A short guide," *Financial Times*, June 7.
88. "Japan robot maker to tackle loneliness with R2-D2-like machine," *Financial Times*, June 7.
89. https://qz.com/709161/its-happening-a-robot-escaped-a-lab-in -russia-and-made-a-dash-for-freedom/, June 16.
90. "Will smarter machines cause mass unemployment?," *The Economist*, June 25.
91. Dewey, Caitlin, "How online bots conned Brexit voters," *The Washington Post*, June 27.
92. Drutman, Lee and Mounk, Yascha, "When the robots rise," *The National Interest*, July 4.

93. "Use of police robot to kill Dallas shooting suspect believed to be first in US history," *The Guardian*, July 8.

94. http://www.fastcompany.com/3061872/the-future-of-work/5-jobs -that-will-be-the-hardest-to-fill-in-2025, July 18, accessed January 9, 2020.

95. Matthews, David, "The robots are coming for the professionals," *Times Higher Education*, July 28.

96. "Sztuczna inteligencja. Miliard pracowników powinno przygotować się na wstrząs," *Gazeta Wyborcza*, August 2.

97. http://www.europeancleaningjournal.com/magazine/articles/ special-feature/the-rise-of-the-robots, August 2, accessed January 9, 2020.

98. https://futurism.com/mall-security-robot-causes-injures-child/, August 4, accessed January 9, 2020.

99. "Dyson 360 Eye vacuum review: the robot that sucks (but in a good way)," *The Guardian*, August 9.

100. "Listen to HAL from '2001' and Samantha from 'Her' talk about their feelings," *Motherboard*, August 15.

101. https://www.dailydot.com/debug/sea-slug-robot-now-a-reality/, accessed August 29, 2016.

102. https://www.weforum.org/agenda/2016/09/jobs-of-future-and-sk ills-you-need, September 2, accessed January 9, 2020.

103. http://www.zeit.de/2016/35/roboter-kuenstliche-intelligenz-anp assung-menschen, September 6, accessed January 9, 2020.

104. "Robots will eliminate 6% of all US jobs by 2021, report says," *The Guardian*, September 14.

105. Avent, Ryan, "A world without work is coming – it could be utopia or it could be hell," The Guardian, September 19.

106. https://finance.yahoo.com/news/u-k-standards-body-issues -182244094.html, September 19, accessed January 9, 2020.

107. http://www.controlengeurope.com/article/124294/Should-we-set -the-robots-free-.aspx, October 3, accessed January 9, 2020.

108. Susskind Richard and Susskind Daniel, "Technology will replace many doctors, lawyers, and other professionals," *Harvard Business Review*, October 11.

109. "Stephen Hawking: AI will be 'either best or worst thing' for humanity," *The Guardian*, October 19.

110. https://singularityhub.com/2016/10/19/8-ways-ai-will-profoundly -change-city-life-by-2030/, accessed January 9, 2020.

111. "Is this economist too far ahead of his time?," *The Chronicle of Higher Education*, October 21.
112. "Sztuczna inteligencja. Bóg już jest," *Gazeta Wyborcza*, October 22.
113. "Made with love – by a robot," *The Washington Post*, November 12.
114. http://www.livescience.com/56887-sci-fi-writing-robot-produces-inspiration,html, November 16, accessed January 9, 2020.
115. "Duke officials test, refine robot-nurse," *Durham News*, November 16.
116. "Den mänskliga roboten Pepper intar Sverige," *Dagens Nyheter*, December 4.
117. "Robot ersätter frånvarande pappa," *Svenska Dagbladet*, December 9.
118. "Världen tar stormsteg mot tänkande maskiner," *Dagens Nyheter*, December 11.
119. "Come Avatar e Aliens ecco i primi passi del robot-umano," *La Repubblica*, December 28.
120. http://www.heraldscotland.com/news/14991269._Robot_revolution_will_put_millions-of_jobs_at_risk_new_report_warns/?ref=ebln, December 29, accessed January 9, 2020.

2017

121. https://www.cbsnews.com/news/60-minutes-autonomous-drones-set-to-revolutionize-military-technology-2/, January 8, accessed January 9, 2020.
122. "Robotskrivna böcker blir allt vanligare," *Göteborgs Posten*, January 10.
123. "Give robots 'personhood' status, EU committee argues," *The Guardian*, January 12.
124. "Was Isaac Asimov a useful idiot for our robot overlords?," *Chicago Tribune*, January 12.
125. https://www.businessinsider.com.au/does-deepminds-ai-experiment-signal-the-start-of-robot-taking-over-jobs-2017-1, January 18, accessed January 9, 2020.
126. http://zeenews.india.com/science/robots-in-newsroom-chinese-robot-reporter-xiao-nan-completes-long-article-in-just-a-second_1968600.html?theme, January 19, accessed January 9, 2020.

127. https://www.rawstory.com/2017/01/scientists-advising-us-military -think-fears-of-robot-apocalypse-are-misguided/, January 20, accessed January 9, 2020.
128. https://www.businessinsider.my/professor-einstein-robot-hanson -robotics-2017-1/, January 22, accessed January 9, 2020.
129. http://robohub.org/factory-move-to-u-s-creates-jobs-with-help -from-robot-workforce/, January 25, accessed January 9, 2020.
130. "How to make America's robots great again," *The New York Times*, January 25.
131. http://www.businessinsider.com/amazons-go-supermarket-of-the -future-3-human-staff-2017-2?r=UK&IR=T&IR=T, February 6, accessed January 9, 2020.
132. https://www.theguardian.com/sustainable-business/2016/nov/ 19/rise-of-the-drones-from-policing-the-streets-to-painting-your -house, accessed February 16, 2017.
133. https://qz.com/911968/bill-gates-the-robot-that-takes-your-job -should-pay-taxes/, February 17, accessed January 9, 2020.
134. Floridi, Luciano, "Roman law offers a better guide to robot rights than sci-fi," *The Financial Times*, February 22.
135. http://www.bbc.co.uk/programmes/articles/ 1R7Bf9rZJyVmFwmXcdNmdHq/seven-sci-fi-predictions-about -robots-that-came-true, February 23, accessed January 9, 2020.
136. http://www.lescienze.it/archivio/articoli/2017/03/01/news/in _difesa_del_robot_disobbediente-3442214/, March 1, accessed January 9, 2020.
137. http://www.barrons.com/articles/rise-of-the-robots-1488609537, March 4, accessed January 9, 2020.
138. https://www.straitstimes.com/singapore/education/race-with -machines-not-against-them, March 6, accessed January 9, 2020.
139. "L'intelligenza artificiale diventa fluida," *Le Scienze*, March 15.
140. http://toronto.citynews.ca/2017/03/30/a-robot-job-invasion-u-s -feds-shrug-it-off-canada-feds-fret-so-whos-right/, March 30, accessed January 9, 2020.
141. "SKF i täten för ny industrirevolution," *Göteborgs Posten*, April 6.
142. http://theconversation.com/to-really-help-us-workers-we-should -invest-in-robots-71125, April 8, accessed January 9, 2020.
143. https://www.cbsnews.com/news/when-the-robots-take-over-will -there-be-jobs-left-for-us/, April 9, accessed January 9, 2020.
144. https://www.weforum.org/agenda/2017/04/why-its-time-to-rethink -the-meaning-of-work/, April 12, accessed January 9, 2020.

145. "Här är roboten som skriver ut en hel byggnad," *Dagens Nyheter*, April 30.

146. http://blogs.faz.net/fazit/2017/05/04/ein-roboter-kostet-sechs -arbeitsplaetze-8673/, May 4, accessed January 9, 2020.

147. https://www.ge.com/digital/blog/dull-dirty-dangerous-its-robot -work, May 14, accessed January 9, 2020.

148. Damm, Darlene, "As machines take jobs, companies need to get creative about making new ones," *Harvard Business Review*, May 22.

149. https://www.indiatimes.com/technology/news/dubai-is-getting-the -world-s-first-robot-police-officer-to-fight-crime-in-a-tech-savvy -manner-322277.html, May 23, accessed January 9, 2020.

150. https://www.sydsvenskan.se/2017-06-01/ingen-mammaledighet -for-dubais-robocop June 1, accessed January 9, 2020.

151. https://www.wired.com/story/san-francisco-just-put-the-brakes-on -delivery-robots/, June 12, accessed January 9, 2020.

152. https://www.weforum.org/agenda/2017/07/how-long-before -a-robot-takes-your-job-here-s-when-ai-experts-think-it-will -happen/, July 26, accessed January 9, 2020.

153. "13 things Apple should automate after driverless cars," *The Guardian*, August 2.

154. https://rodneybrooks.com/forai-domo-arigato-mr-roboto/, August 28, accessed January 9, 2020.

155. "Deutsche Bank boss says 'big number' of staff will lose jobs to automation," *The Guardian*, September 6.

156. https://rodneybrooks.com/the-seven-deadly-sins-of-predicting-the -future-of-ai/, September 7, accessed January 9, 2020.

157. https://www.welt.de/wirtschaft/article169640579/Kuestliche -Intelligenz-macht-denDeutschen-Angst.html, October 15, accessed January 9, 2020.

158. https://www.forbes.com/forbes/welcome/?toURL=https://www .forbes.com/sites/bernardmarr/2017/10/16/the-4-ds-of-robotization -dull-dirty-dangerous-and-dear/2/&refURL=&referrer= #529b152917c4, accessed January 9, 2020.

159. https://www.wired.com/story/americans-love-automation-when-it -costs-someone-else-a-job/, October 17, accessed January 9, 2020.

160. "Digital transformation will be dramatic and painful," *The Financial Times*, October 26.

161. http://theconversation.com/an-ai-professor-explains-three
-concerns-about-granting-citizenship-to-robot-Sophia-86479,
October 30, accessed January 9, 2020.
162. https://futurism.com/boston-dynamics-ceo-believes-robotics
-bigger-internet/, November 15, accessed January 9, 2020.
163. "Undervattensrobot ska sanera miljöbomb," *Göteborgs Posten*,
November 17.
164. "Jobben du inte visste var hotade av AI," *Svenska Dagbladet*,
November 17.
165. http://thenerdstash.com/robot-passes-medical-exam/,   November
19, accessed January 9, 2020.
166. http://www.faz.net/aktuell/wissen/computer-mathematik/deutscher
-zukunftspreis-fuer-smartes-helferlein-verliehen-15317809.html,
November 30, accessed January 9, 2020.
167. Madrigal, Alexis C., "Should children form emotional bonds with
robots?," *The Atlantic*, December.
168. https://nordic.businessinsider.com/swedish-robot-guru-these-are
-the-crucial-skills-to-survive-when-ai-butchers-the-job-market--,
December 1, accessed January 9, 2020.
169. "Robot mer försiktig än en mänsklig sjuksköterska," *Svenska
Dagbladet*, December 2.
170. "Bilder visar robot som hotar USA," *Svenska Dagbladet*, December
2.
171. "Om vi klantar till det med artificiell intelligens kan vi ha sabbat
hela mänsklighetens framtid om 40 år," *Dagens Nyheter*, December
3.
172. "Arriva Sam, il primo politico robot. Vuole candidarsi nel 2020 in
Nuova Zelanda," *La Repubblica*, December 4.
173. "Varannan redo för robotchef," *Svenska Dagbladet*, December 10.
174. https://moneymorning.com/2017/12/12/the-real-robot-invasion
-is-here-find-out-how-to-profit-from-it/, December 12, accessed
January 9, 2020.
175. https://www.nbcnews.com/mach/science/5-star-technologies
-now-moving-make-believe-reality-ncna828906, December 13,
accessed January 9, 2020.

Bibliography

2001: A Space Odyssey. (1968) Metro-Goldwyn-Mayer, screenplay Stanley Kubrick and Arthur C. Clarke, directed by Stanley Kubrick.

Acemoglu, Daron and Autor, David (2011) Skills, tasks and technologies: Implications for employment and earnings. In: Ashenfelter, Orley, Layard, Richard, Layard, Baron and Card, David (eds) *Handbook of labor economics*, Vol. 4b. Amsterdam: Elsevier, 1044–1171.

Anslow, Louis (2016) Robots have been about to take all the jobs for more than 200 years. May 16. https://timeline.com/robots-have-been-about-to-take-all -the-jobs-for-more-than-200-years-5c9c08a2f41d (accessed November 29, 2017).

Asimov, Isaac (1950/1996) *I, Robot.* London: HarperCollins

Asimov, Isaac (1981) *Asimov on science fiction.* New York: Doubleday & Co.

Baldwin, Richard (2019) *The globotic upheaval: Globalization, robotics and the future of work.* New York: Oxford University Press.

Bank of America Merrill Lynch (2015) Robot revolution – Global robot & AI primer. http://www.bofaml.com/content/dam/boamlimages/documents/PDFs/ robotics_and_ai_condensed_primer.pdf (accessed July 18, 2016).

Bauman, Zygmunt (2017) *Retrotopia.* Cambridge: Polity Press.

de Beauvoir, Simone (1949) *Le deuxiéme sexe.* Paris: Gallimard.

Berner, Boel (1996) *Sakernas tillstånd.* Kön, klass, teknisk expertis. Stockholm: Carlssons.

Big Hero 6 (2014) Disney; screenplay by Steven T. Seagle and Duncan Rouleau, directed by Don Hall and Chris Williams.

Blade Runner (1982) Warner Bros., based on a novel by Philip K. Dick, directed by Ridley Scott.

Bloomfield, Brian P. (2003) Narrating the future of intelligent machines: The role of science fiction in technological anticipation. In: Czarniawska, Barbara and Gagliardi, Pasquale (eds) *Narratives we organize by.* Amsterdam: John Benjamins, 193–212.

Boström, Nick (2014) *Superintelligence: Paths, dangers, strategies.* Oxford: Oxford University Press.

Bowler, Peter J. (2017) *A history of the future: Prophets of progress from H.G. Wells to Isaac Asimov.* Cambridge: Cambridge University Press.

Bradbury, Malcolm (2000) *To the hermitage.* London: Picador.

Braverman, Harry (1974) *Labor and monopoly capital: The degradation of work in the twentieth century.* New York: Monthly Review Press.

Brito, Dagobert and Curl, Robert (2015) Income inequality and social mobility. http://bakerinstitute.org/research/turing-robots-income-inequality-and-social -mobility/ (accessed July 18, 2016).

Brooks, Christopher K. (1988) "More human than human": In search of human condition. *Journal of American Culture*, 11(4): 65–71.

Brynjolfsson, Erik and McAfee, Andrew (2011) *Race against the machine*. Lexington, MA: Digital Frontier Press.

Brynjolfsson, Erik and McAfee, Andrew (2014/2016) *The second machine age: Work, progress, and prosperity in a time of brilliant technologies*. New York: W.W. Norton.

Bullaro, Grace Russo (1993) Blade Runner: The subversion and redefinition of categories. *Riverside Quarterly*, 9(2): 102–108.

Burenstam Linder, Stefan (1970) *The harried leisure class*. New York: Columbia University Press.

Bütepage, Judith and Kragic, Danica (2017) Human-robot collaboration: From psychology to social robotics. https://arxiv.org/pdf/1705.10146.pdf (accessed November 30, 2017).

Cameron, Nigel M. de S. (2017) *Will robots take your job? A plea for consensus*. Cambridge: Polity.

Čapek, Karel (1990) *Toward the radical center. A Karel Čapek reader*. Edited by Peter Kussi. North Haven, CT: Catbird Press.

Chaboud, Alain P., Chiquoine, Benjamin, Hjalmarsson, Erik and Vega, Clara (2014) Rise of the machines: Algorithmic trading in the foreign exchange market. *The Journal of Finance*, 69(5): 2045–2084.

Cockburn, Cynthia (1996) Hushållsteknik: Askungen och ingenjörerna. In: Sundin, Elisabeth and Berner, Boel (eds) *Från symaskin till cyborg: Genus, teknik och social förändring*. Stockholm: Nerenius & Santérus, 19–41.

Cohen, Michael D., March, James G. and Olsen, Johan P. (1972) A garbage can model of organizational choice. *Administrative Science Quarterly*, 17(1): 1–25.

Coleman, A.M. (1936) The accountant in literature. *Notes and Queries*, June 13, p. 428.

Cowan, Ruth Schwartz (1985) *More work for mother: The ironies of household technology from the open hearth to the microwave*. New York: Basic Books.

Crevier, Daniel (1993) *AI: The tumultuous search for artificial intelligence*. New York: Basic Books.

Czarniawska, Barbara (2010) The construction of businesswoman in the media: Between evil and frailty. In: Chouliaraki, Lilie and Morsing, Mette (eds) *Media, organizations and identity*. London: Palgrave, 185–208.

Czarniawska, Barbara (2012) Accounting and detective stories: An excursion to the USA in the 1940s. *Accounting, Auditing & Accountability Journal*, 25(4): 659–672.

Czarniawska, Barbara (2013) Is speed good? *Scandinavian Journal of Management*, 29: 7–12.

Czarniawska, Barbara (2019) Virtual red tape, or digital v. paper bureaucracy. In: Czarniawska, Barbara and Löfgren, Orvar (eds) *Overwhelmed by overflows?* Lund: Lund University Press, 170–190.

Czarniawska, Barbara and Gustavsson, Eva (2008) The (d)evolution of the cyber-woman? *Organization*, 15(5): 655-683.

Czarniawska, Barbara, and Rhodes, Carl (2006) Strong plots: Popular culture in management practice and theory. In: Gagliardi, Pasquale and Czarniawska, Barbara (eds) *Management education and humanities*. Cheltenham, UK and Northampton, MA, USA: Edward Elgar Publishing, 195–218.

Czarniawska, Barbara and Solli, Rolf (2019) *The future welfare in Sweden*. Paper presented at the NFF Conference, Vaasa, August 22–24.

Devlin, Kate (2019) *Turned on: Science, sex and robots*. London: Bloomsbury.

Dick, Philip K. (1968) *Do androids dream of electric sheep*. New York: Ballantine Books.

Dick, Philip K. (1976/1995) Man, android and machine. In: Sutin, Lawrence (ed.) *The shifting realities of Philip K. Dick. Selected literary and philosophical writings*. New York: Pantheon, 211–232.

Diebold, John (1952) *Automation. The advent of the automatic factory*. New York: D. Van Nostrand.

Edge (2015) What do you think about machines that think? https://www.edge .org/annual-question/what-do-you-think-about-machines-that-think (accessed January 6, 2018).

Ehrenreich, Barbara and Hochschild, Arlie Russell (eds) (2002) *The global woman*. London: Granta.

Eriksson-Zetterquist, Ulla (2008) Living with the myth of unattainable technology. In: Kostera, Monika (ed.) *Organizational epics and sagas*. London: Palgrave, 26–39.

Executive Office of the President of the United States (2016) Artificial intelligence, automation, and the economy, December. https://obamawhitehouse .archives.gov/sites/whitehouse.gov/files/documents/Artificial-Intelligence -Automation-Economy.PDF (accessed November 30, 2017).

Ex Machina (2015) Universal Pictures, screenplay and director Alex Garland.

Fleming, Peter (2018) Robots and organization studies: Why robots might not want to steal your job. *Organization Studies*, 40(1): 23–28.

Floridi, Luciano (2002) *Philosophy and computing: An introduction*. Abington: Taylor & Francis.

Floridi, Luciano (2014) *The 4th revolution: How the infosphere is reshaping human reality*. Oxford: Oxford University Press.

Fölster, Stefan (2014) *Vartannat jobb automatiseras inom 20 år – utmaningar för Sverige*. Stockholm: Stiftelse för strategisk forskning.

Ford, Martin (2015) *The rise of the robots: Technology and the threat of mass unemployment*. London: Oneworld Publications.

Frennert, Susanne (2016) *Older people meet robots*. Lund: Lund University Press.

Frey, Carl Benedikt and Osborne, Michael A. (2013) The future of employment: How susceptible are jobs to computerisation? http://www.oxfordmartin.ox.ac .uk/publications/view/1314 (accessed July 18, 2016).

Grace, Katja, Salvatier, John, Dafoe, Allan, Zhang, Baobao and Evans, Ovain (2017) *When will AI exceed human performance? Evidence from AI experts*. arXiv:1705.08807v2 [cs.AI] May 30, 2017.

Greenman, Andrew (2008) Brand new talk: Constructing fashionability in a consulting trend. *International Studies of Management & Organization*, 38(2): 44–70.

Greer, John Michael (2016) *Retrotopia*. Danville, IL: Founders House Publishing.

Gustavsson, Eva and Czarniawska, Barbara (2004) Web woman: The on-line construction of corporate and gender images. *Organization*, 11(5): 651–670.

Haagh, Louise (2019) *The case for universal basic income*. Cambridge: Polity Press.

Hayles, Katherine N. (1994) Boundary disputes: Homeostasis, reflexivity and the foundations of cybernetics. *Configurations*, 3: 441–467.

Hayles, Katherine N. (2005) Computing the human. *Theory, Culture & Society*, 22(1): 131–151.

Interstellar (2014), Warner Bros, written by Jonathan and Christopher Nolan, directed by Christopher Nolan.

Joerges, Bernward (1989) Romancing the machine – reflections on the social scientific construction of computer reality. *International Studies of Management and Organization*, 19(4): 24–50.

Joerges, Bernward (1996) *Leinwanstädte. Vorüberlegungen zu einer Soziologie der gefilmten Stadt.* https://www.wzb.eu/www2000/alt/met/pdf/ leinwandstaedte.pdf (accessed November 26, 2017).

Joerges, Bernward and Kress, Dorothea (2002) Dual cities. Das Motiv der "geteilten Stadt" zwischen Stadtfilm und Stadtsoziologie. In: Wilhelm, Karin and Langenbrinck, Gregor (eds) *City-Lights – Zentren, Peripherien, Regionen. Interdisziplinäre Positionen für eine urabne Kultur.* Wien: Böhlau Verlag, 88–104.

Johnson, Richard (1986–87) What is cultural studies anyway? *Social Text*, 16: 38–80.

Krieg, Peter (1988) *Machine dreams*. Berlin: Barefoot Production.

Kurzweil, Raymond (2005) *The Singularity is near. When humans transcend biology*. New York: Viking.

Latour, Bruno (1987) The enlightenment without critique: A word on Michel Serres' philosophy. In: Griffith, A. Phillips (ed.) *Contemporary French philosophy*. Cambridge: Cambridge University Press, 83–97.

Latour, Bruno (1993) *We have never been modern*. Cambridge, MA: Harvard University Press.

Levin, Ira (1972/2002) *The Stepford wives*. New York: HarperCollins.

Liljefors, Max, Noll, Gregor and Steuert, Daniel (2019) *War and algorithm*. Lanham, MR: Rowman and Littlefield International.

Liljefors, Noomi and Sundgren, Mats (2003) Bröder i brott. *GöteborgsPosten*, January 23.

Lin, Tom C.W. (2013) The new investor. *60 UCLA LAW Review*, 678–735.

MacDorman, Karl F. and Ishiguro, Hiroshi (2006) The uncanny advantage of using androids in social and cognitive science research. *Interaction Studies*, 7(3): 297–337.

Marsh, Henry (2019) Can man ever build a mind? *Financial Times*, January 10, https://www.ft.com/content/2e75c04a-0f43-11e9-acdc-4d9976f1533b, accessed January 17 2020.

McAfee, Andrew and Brynjolfssson, Erik (2017) *Machine, platform, crowd: Harnessing our digital future.* New York: W.W. Norton & Company.

McDowell, Linda (1997) *Capital culture: Gender at work in the city.* Oxford: Blackwell.

McKinsey Global Institute (2017) *A future that works: Automation, employment and productivity.* January.

McLuhan, Marshall (1964/1994) *Understanding media: The extension of man.* Cambridge, MA: MIT Press.

Meinecke, Lisa and Voss, Laura (2018) "I robot, you unemployed": Science-fiction and robotics in the media. In: Engelschalt, Julia, Maibaum, Arne, Engels, Franziska and Odenwald, Jakob (eds) *Schafft Wissen – Gemeinsames und geteiltes Wissen in Wissenschaft und Technik.* INSIST-Proceedings 2; October 7–8, 2016, München, 203–215.

Metz, David (2003) From naked emperor to Count Zero. Tracking knights, nerds, and cyberpunks in identity narratives of freelancers in the IT-field. In: Czarniawska, Barbara and Gagliardi, Pasquale (eds) *Narratives we organize by.* Amsterdam: John Benjamins, 173–192.

Miller, Arthur (1990) Foreword. *Toward the radical center. A Karel Čapek reader* (edited by Peter Kussi). North Haven, CT: Catbird Press, i–vi.

Minsky, Marvin L. (1966) Artificial intelligence. *Scientific American,* 215(3): 246–263.

Moore, Fiona (2016) *Seal.* In: Trenholm, Hayden and Rimar, Michael (eds) *Lazarus risen,* Toronto: Bundoran Press, 91–104.

Moore, Fiona (2018) *Driving ambitions.* Toronto: Bundoran Press.

Moravec, Hans (1988) *Mind children: Future of robot and human intelligence.* Cambridge, MA: Harvard University Press.

Morozov, Evgeny (2012) A robot stole my Pulitzer! How automated journalism and loss of reading privacy may hurt civil discourse. *Slate,* March 19. https://slate.com/technology/2012/03/narrative-science-robot-journalists-customized-news-and-the-danger-to-civil-discourse.html (accessed May 7, 2019).

Morozov, Evgeny (2013) *To save everything, click here: The folly of technological solutionism.* New York: PublicAffairs.

Muro, Mark, Maxim, Robert and Whiton, Jacob (2019) *Automation and artificial intelligence. How machines are affecting people and places.* New York: Metropolitan Policy Program at Brookings.

Nordin, Peter and Wilde, Johanna (2003) *Humanoider. Självlärande robotar och artificiell intelligens.* Stockholm: Liber.

OECD (2018) *Automation, skills use and training.* https://www.oecd-ilibrary.org/employment/automation-skills-use-and-training_2e2f4eea-en;jsessionid=0Yb9yxOuW2sHbUQY6gx6ZpFZ.ip-10-240-5-172 (accessed June 3, 2019).

Parker, Martin (1998) Judgment Day: Cyborganization, humanism and postmodern ethics, *Organization,* 5(4): 503–518.

Parker, Martin, Higgins, Matthew, Lightfoot, Geoff and Smith, Warren (eds) (1999/2007) *Science fiction and organizations.* London: Routledge.

Pickering, Andrew (2010) *The cybernetic brain. Sketches of another future.* Chicago: University of Chicago Press.

Piketty, Thomas (2014) *Capital in the twenty-first century.* Cambridge, MA: Belknap Press.

Poe, Edgar Allan (1836) Maelzel's chess player. http:en.wikipedia.org/wiki/ Maelzel%27s–Chess–Player (accessed November 30, 2017).

Rappe, Tinni Ernsjöö and Strannegård, Lars (2004) *Rent hus. Slaget om den svenska dammråttan.* Stockholm: Norstedts.

Reichardt, Jasia (1978) *Robots: Facts, fiction, and prediction.* London: Penguin.

Rhodes, Carl and Brown, Andrew B. (2005) Writing responsibly: narrative fiction and organization studies. *Organization,* 12(4): 467–491.

Riskin, Jessica (2016) *The restless clock: A history of the centuries-long argument over what makes living things tick.* Chicago, IL: University of Chicago Press.

Schor, Juliet B. (1991) *The overworked American.* New York: Basic Books.

Scott, James C. (1998) *Seeing like a state.* New Haven, CT: Yale University Press.

Searle, John R. (2014) What your computer can't know. *The New York Review of Books,* October 9.

Shields, Charles J. (2011) *And so it goes: Kurt Vonnegut: A life.* New York: St. Martin's Griffin.

Smith, Aaron and Anderson, Janna (2014) AI, robotics, and the future of jobs. http://www.pewinternet.org/2014/08/06/future-of-jobs/ (accessed July 18, 2016).

Sofge, Erik (2014) The co-robots in "Interstellar" are gorgeous – and silly. *Popular Science,* October 27. http://www.popsci.com/article/technology/co -robots-interstellar-are-gorgeous-and-silly (accessed March 31, 2017).

Sone, Yuji (2017) *Japanese robot culture. Performance, imagination, and modernity.* New York: Palgrave Macmillan.

Star Wars (First Trilogy) (1977–1980) 20th Century Fox, directed by George Lucas.

Stephenson, Neal (1992) *Snow crash.* New York: Bantam Books.

Stephenson, Neal (2015) *Seveneves.* New York: HarperCollins.

Stone, Tobias (2016) *History tells us what will happen next.* https://medium .com/@theonlytoby/history-tells-us-what-will-happen-next-with-brexit-trump -a3fefd154714#.vwqv11fxq (accessed July 27, 2016).

Street, John (1997) *Politics and popular culture.* Oxford: Blackwell.

Sunstein, Cass R. (2016) *The world according to Star Wars.* New York: HarperCollins.

Tarde, Gabriel (1896/1905) *Underground man.* London: Duckworth and Co.

Tasker, Yvonne (2013) Women in film noir. In: Spicer, Andrew and Hanson, Helen (eds) *A companion to film noir.* Hoboken, NJ: Wiley, 353–352.

The Matrix (1999) Silver Pictures Production, screenwriters and directors: Larry and Andy Wachowski.

The National Academies of Sciences, Engineering & Medicine (2017) *Information technology and the U.S. workforce. Where are we and where do we go from here?* Washington, DC: The National Academies Press. https://doi.org/10 .17226/24649.

The Stepford Wives (1975) Palomar Pictures and Fadsin Cinema Associates, screenplay: William Goldman, director: Bryan Forbes.

The Stepford Wives (2004) DreamWorks L.L.C. and Paramount Pictures Corporation, screenplay: Paul Rudnick, director: Frank Oz.

Traube, Elizabeth G. (1992) *Dreaming identities: Class, gender and generation in 1980s Hollywood movies.* Boulder, CO: Westview Press.

Turner, Stephen (2014) Mundane theorizing, bricolage and Bildung. In: Swedberg, Richard (ed.) *Theorizing in social science. The context of discovery.* Stanford, CA: Stanford University Press, 131–137.

Varese, Federico (2004) Great mobility. *Times Literary Supplement*, July 2, 6–7.

Vonnegut, Kurt (1952) *Player piano.* New York: Scribner.

Weick, Karl E. (1995) *Sensemaking in organizations.* Thousand Oaks, CA: Sage.

White, Hayden (1998) *The content of the form. Narrative discourse and historical representation.* Baltimore, MD: The John Hopkins University Press.

Whyte, William (1956) *The organization man.* New York: Simon and Schuster.

Williams, Douglas E. (2017) Ideology as dystopia: An interpretation of "Blade Runner," *Scraps from the Loft*, July 6. http://scrapsfromtheloft.com/2017/07/06/ideology-dystopia-interpretation-blade-runner/ (accessed November 7, 2017).

World Economic Forum (2016) The future of jobs: Employment, skills and workforce strategy for the fourth industrial revolution. http://reports.weforum.org/future-of-jobs-2016/ (accessed January 6, 2018).

Index